'HIGH ON THE HILL'
A HISTORY OF TRURO SCHOOL

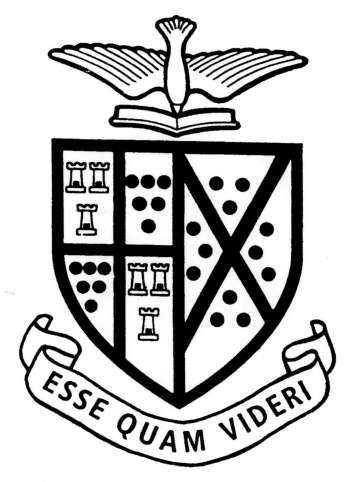

ESSE QUAM VIDERI

1880-2004

'HIGH ON THE HILL'
A HISTORY OF TRURO SCHOOL

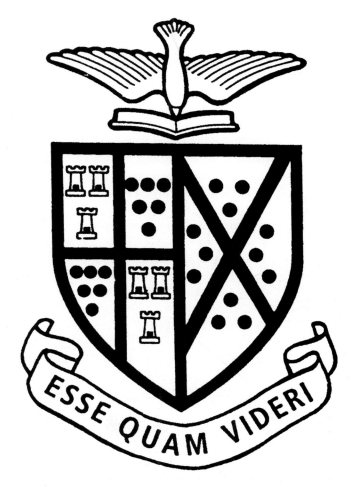

ESSE QUAM VIDERI

1880-2004

BY JOANNA WOOD
BLUE HILLS PUBLISHING

This book was the idea of Don Castling, to whose memory it is dedicated. Don was an old boy of the school and former chairman of the Truro School Former Pupils' Association.

First published in Great Britain in 2005
by Blue Hills Publishing, St Austell
for the Truro School Former Pupils' Association, Truro School,
Trennick Lane, Truro, TR1 1TH.
Tel: 01872 272763
website: www.truroschool.com

Copyright © Joanna Wood
Front Cover: Photograph of Truro School from Lemon Quay c.1900 (© Royal Cornwall Museum TEqbt007)
Back cover: Photograph of Truro School c.1886 (© Royal Cornwall Museum TEsch151)

ISBN 0-9549005-1-0

Designed by Louise Hillier Designs, St Agnes.

Printed and bound by T.J. International Ltd., Padstow

Contents

Foreword

We are indeed lucky that one hundred and twenty-five years ago the Methodist Conference decided to build a school in Truro and chose such a wonderful site, high above the city. The Truro School Former Pupils' Association has prepared this comprehensive history of the school in celebration of this significant anniversary.

Truro School has always prided itself on providing the best education and sports training in the Duchy of Cornwall and in its first one hundred and twenty-five years more than ten thousand pupils have been educated there. Some have become famous, but most have not: many have been successful but some have not. Nevertheless, most of us would agree that during our days at school we learned many things about life and people that equipped us to meet future challenges, and we made many friendships that are valued still.

With this book we hope to bring back some good memories for those who were directly involved in the events described and to interest anyone who can relate to them. George Heyworth and Bill Williams, both members of the current T.S.F.P.A. committee, recall their early days at the school towards the end of the war years and rationing:

For a small boy it was a strict regime. One remembers the prefects, the roll calls, the supervised preps and the punishments. We still wore mortar boards and black jackets to march to church through the city on Sundays. We still wore indoor and outdoor shoes. We had our tuck shop, our school clubs, school trips, sports days, speech days, school plays and Sunday chapel. All of this moulded us into what we are today. It was a happy and contented life surrounded by loyal friends and a most respected, friendly staff.

These were days of great privation; food and fuel were still rationed and the tuck shop had very limited goodies. However, like most new pupils, I soon developed a great pride and satisfaction in becoming a pupil at the school. Dr Magson was a strict disciplinarian and much respected by all the boys and members of staff. His deputy, Mr Willday, was a much loved 'Mr Chips' figure. Mrs Magson played a great role on the spiritual side and persuaded many of us to become members of her Bible class. She failed however to persuade me to join 'The White Ribbon Society', aimed at total abstinence for life. I found her garden, below the tennis court, a much greater attraction and paid many visits over the years, scrumping for apples and gooseberries. Only one period during my seven years I remember with sorrow – the polio epidemic of 1947 when three pupils died, including a close friend in my year.

Hopefully the vast majority of us can look back on our schooldays with such good memories, and memories mean a great deal more if shared. We believe you will find this book of lasting value and perhaps it will prompt a few to contact old friends who you have not seen for many years. Life is all about friendships and some of the best friends you will ever make were those made at school.

This book was the idea of Don Castling, who sadly died in March 2004 before seeing it published. If it prompts people to contact old friends from school Don would have been pleased.

Truro School Former Pupils' Association Committee, January 2005

Opposite page - photograph © rcm TEqbt007

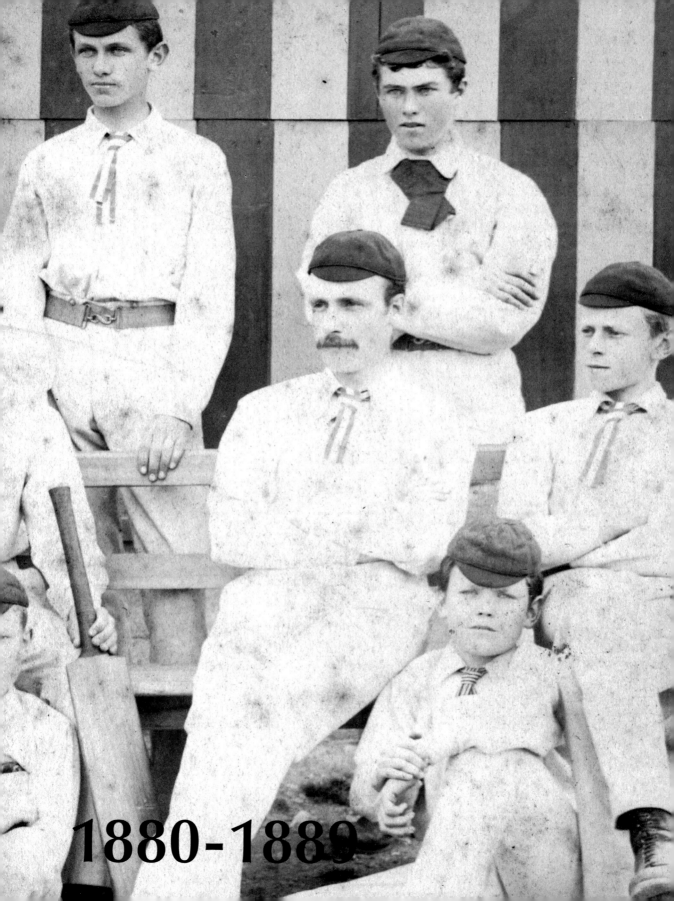

1880-1880

1880 – 1889: 'The Pioneer Years'

On Tuesday 20 January 1880 thirty-five boys, several of whom wanted a good night's rest, sat down to lessons for the first time in the newly opened Truro College. The lessons took place in a schoolroom adjoining the Congregational Chapel in River Street. The previous day the Truro Wesleyan Middle Class College had been formally opened with much ceremony, incorporating the dedication performed by Reverend Benjamin Gregory, President of the Wesleyan Conference, assisted by Reverend Hugh Jones, chairman of the Methodist District, and Mr W. Bickford-Smith, the chairman of the school directors. Problems were already occurring when on the first night in the boarding house at 4 Strangways Terrace, the beds had not been delivered on time and boarders had to sleep on makeshift beds until they arrived[1].

The origins of Truro School lie in the Wesleyan Methodist Conference of 1878 and the Victorian movement for wider education. By the late nineteenth century, Wesleyan Methodism, compared to the other branches of Methodism, was the mainstream division and predominantly a middle class phenomenon, contrasting with the Primitive Methodists and Bible Christians whose ethics appealed to the respectable working class. The Conference, held in Bradford, was the first time that laymen participated fully with ministers in the meeting. Consequently this occasion was celebrated through the collection of a 'Thanksgiving Fund'. Out of the amount raised through generous donations, £10,000 was assigned to the foundation of middle class schools[2]. This in turn led to the foundation of the Truro Wesleyan Middle Class College, which was one of four Methodist secondary schools opened between 1870 and 1885. Dunheved College in Launceston opened in 1873, and Truro College in 1880, were both boys' schools; while Redbrooke College in Camborne opened in 1879, and West Cornwall College in Penzance opened in 1883, for girls' education[3].

The second half of the nineteenth century witnessed increased education legislation. Truro College was founded on the basis of this; in particular Forster's Act of 1870, which included the ruling that education must be provided for all children under the age of thirteen, and Sandon's Act passed in 1876, under which all children had to attend school up to the age of ten. By the time the College had been open for several months, another Act was in place whereby parents and school boards had to ensure that children attended school. The potential difficulties presented by these acts were overcome because the College was a fee-paying private school, with twenty-five of the initial intake of pupils attending as boarders. The educational reform that was taking place nationally shared

The schoolroom of the Bethesda Congregational Chapel in River Street, Truro, where lessons were first held in 1880

many similarities with the Methodist ethos. The Liberal Party attracted Methodist support, which is reflected in the educational acts passed under their administration[4]. Like John Wesley in the eighteenth century, they were attempting to make education available to the masses. The foundation of Truro College could be seen as bridge between old an new; it was born out of the educational movement and set up as a business instead of relying on a charitable organisation, but like older schools was set up by an independent body, with its own religious philosophy.

Methodism reinforced the nineteenth-century view that there was a close connection between education and religion. John Wesley called for the education of children and adults so that his preachers would not be illiterate or ignorant, being well aware of the dangers that ignorance could create. However at the same time he was equally aware of the excesses of too much sophistication and the influence of fashion. Consequently a balance was needed between the two, to make well-rounded individuals. The overall aim, therefore, was to provide education 'in the nurture and admonition of the Lord'[5].

The years around 1880 were also a turning point in Truro's history: the cathedral was being built for the newly formed diocese, while trade was slowing down, leading to the closure of the port. The town was again evolving, losing some of its old functions but gaining impetus from its new status as a cathedral city[6]. It is has been thought that Truro School was founded as a reaction and show of strength in response to the building of the cathedral and the creation of the Cornish diocese; '...the restoration of the Cornish See was expected to cause a considerable Anglican upsurge and it was thought appropriate that the Wesleyans should have their venture of faith too'[7]. It is just as likely that the Anglican Church wanted to reassert their existence in a county that was being nicknamed the 'Methodist County'[8].

In 1879 the Cornish Methodist Connexion met to discuss the formation of a school in Truro. A board of company directors, for the Cornwall Wesleyan Methodist School Association (Ltd), was set up with Mr W. Bickford-Smith, of Trevarno, as the chairman, and the headmaster was appointed - George Owen Turner, from Dunheved College, who would live at the school with his young family[9]. Several of the first pupils were the sons of the directors, reflecting the need that was felt for a Cornish middle-class boarding school, and the direct involvement of parents in its establishment and direction. The school therefore began its life in River Street, though its ostensible address was 4 Strangways Terrace. It soon became clear that the number of boarders would be overflowing from the house before too long, so in the following year another house was acquired for boarding space in Lemon Street; thought to be number 7. This was to prove adequate only for a short time; it was not long before purpose-built school buildings were though necessary. The Lemon Street boarding house 'with a front bedroom conveniently opposite a public lamp'[10]. was not ideal for the master and boys who had to live there.

4 Strangways Terrace, the first home of the school

The school's aim was to provide an education fit for a middle class boy, whether classical or commercial, to enable further study or to enter a trade, combined with a 'foundation of truth, the principle of all Christian morality', which it was thought 'alone can make a worthy British Citizen'[11]. Mr Turner, with his assistant Mr W. Vincent gave their pupils groundings in English, arithmetic, Latin, and the humanities; it was not until the premises and number of teachers grew that more subjects could be taught. Mr E. Holt was appointed the first music master in 1881. Exercise or sports were also incorporated into the pupils' day. Number 4 Strangways Terrace 'became the centre of light and leading to many Cornish lads'[12]. There was an increased feeling of identity and distinctiveness when the school motto, 'esse quam videri', and school crest were introduced in late 1880[13]. It now became the aspiration of all who passed through the school to live up to the ideal of 'being rather than seeming to be'.

Early memories of the school in Strangways Terrace included the 'perpetual smell of tan' that pervaded and the lack of grass in the play area, which was so small that before long every corner of the garden was well known by pupils and teachers alike. Turner recalled several years later, that despite the difficulties inseparable from the start, life then was very enjoyable, 'though not a pupil knew how to work a vulgar fraction, though little more than the three Rs so called had crossed their mental horizon, though many a Cornishism would buzz through the air, the uncorrectness of which, when pointed out, would shake their simple faith in the old county and show them that the world was bigger than any part of it, by no means an axiom to a boy'[14].

The first prize day was held in December 1880. Prizes were given for English, Mathematics, and Bible class, as well as to the class leaders, improvers and for excellence in examination, which went to H.

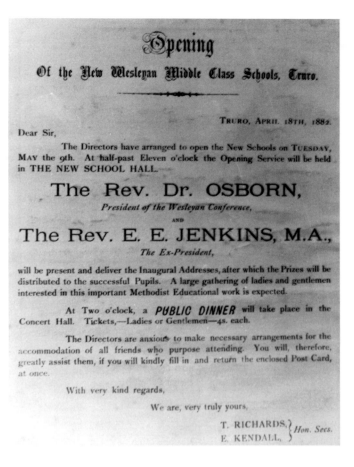

A notice for the opening of the school at the present site in 1882. The Rev. Dr Osborn was a former headmaster of Kingswood School and had been connected Truro College since the beginning

Mitchell for his 3rd class result[15]. The first successes in the Cambridge Local Examinations took place in 1881, and the prizes that year were presented by George J. Smith of Treliske, who established the Smith-Dunheved Annual Scholarship in 1883, allowing the holder to one year's training at Dunheved College[16].

Once again it was not long before new accommodation was required. The directors had been offered a piece of land, on a hill on the eastern side of the city, called Nicoll's Estate. It was thought the new position of the school would relieve parents' anxieties to find 'the safest, healthiest and best school' for their children[17]. A competition was opened for architects to design plans for the new

School photograph from c.1885. George Turner, headmaster 1880-1887 sits between his wife Mary Eliza Turner and H.W. Vinter. (copyright Royal Cornwall Museum TEsch152)

building, with a prize of £25. Mr Elliot Etwell of West Bromwich won the prize out of twelve entrants from around the country. The building contract was given to Julian and Sons of Truro, who erected the building for a coast of £5,165 using local stone quarried down the hill from the school[18]. The building was described as '...a free treatment of the Gothic, and is divided into three sections, a central block with two wings. The central portion and the right wing are devoted to the school and administrative purposes, whilst the left wing will comprise the residence of the headmaster, servants' apartments, and kitchen'[19].

On 7 June 1881, after a procession and service in St Mary's Chapel, the Lord Mayor of London, the Right Honarable W.A. McArthur, laid the foundation stone of the new school building. In his address, McArthur asserted to the audience that the times in which they were living was 'pre-eminently an era of education, and one of the most satisfacto-

ry phases of the movement, is the manner in which religious education is being brought to the front …', proving to be more beneficial than secular education, which failed to realise 'an harmonious and equable evolution of the human powers'[20]. The ceremony closed with a concert given by the Royal Marines and fireworks at the school site.

By the spring of 1882 the new building was ready for 70 boarders and 30 day-pupils. 'Matters long dreamt of began slowly to shape themselves; sports became more interesting and appreciated, various school societies sprang into existence, masters left and masters came, and before long the present Head Master, Mr H.W. Vinter, … joined the School staff …'[21]. Herbert Vinter joined the staff in 1883. By this time the teaching staff had increased to seven, including a drawing master and drill instructor[22]. Physical development to the school also continued, with the carriage drive and terraces laid out in front of the school in December 1883. Vinter recalled that 'I believe a baker's cart was the first vehicle to appear on the new road'; it had been planned that it would first be used for the arrival of the Conference President the following term[23].

Henry Rosewarne became a boarder in the first term that Truro College occupied its new premises. Among his memories of these early days was the tale of several schoolboy pranks, which included beeswaxing the place of a certain boy on a bench in the Dining Room, so the boy stuck fast and Matron had to cut out the seat of his trousers with scissors to free him. This was much to the amusement of Mr Turner's niece who was staying at the school at the time; this practical joke resulted in light punishment only.

The dormitories were known as top front, bottom front, top back and bottom back. At one stage Henry was a prefect for the bottom back dormitory and was caused much anxiety by a boy who walked in his sleep, and one night attempted to climb out of a window. The master sleeping next door was 'the type who would be likely to panic and spoil everything', so using his own initiative Henry managed to get the boy back in with the help of others in the dormitory. He also remembered the tale of the forcible scrubbing of a boy who never washed[24].

Several former pupils had family connections to the early days of the school. A letter from T.W.M. Darlington about his time at Truro School in the 1930s, referred to the washing of school clothes for boarders in the 1880s[25]. His grandfather, who drove a horse-drawn bus, used to transport the school laundry to the 'laundry lady', called Eathorne, who lived at Greensplat near Frogpool in the late 1870s and early 1880s. J. McCoskrie, writing in 1955, recalled that his grandfather Frederick McCoskrie was number one on the roll call when the school first opened and was 'a form of senior prefect'. At

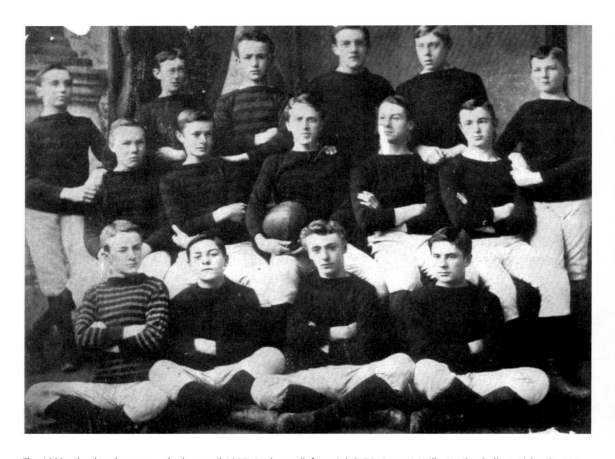

The 1882 school rugby team – the last until 1930. Back row (left to right): F.R. Bate, H. Wills, H. Chenhalls, J. Richards, C.H. Tillman, H. Sleep. Middle row: C. Cloke, R.S. Boyns, E. Boyns, S.J. Cranford, R.S. Rundle. Front row: T.Chenhalls, J.H. Trounson; it is not clear who the last two are

the first old boys' dinner in 1905, Edward Wilton, who was at the school in Strangways Terrace in 1880, claimed the distinction of being the oldest old boy, as he was the first to leave[26].

The Devon and Cornwall Wesleyan Elementary Day School scholarship was founded in January 1887, which made a private education more accessible. Three boys at Truro College, W.J. Tolley, Penrose and Ball, benefited from the scholarship for two years each, and went on to achieve academic success. This scholarship helped to dismiss the apparent paradoxical nature of a Methodist private boarding school; because a private school in theory went against the belief of education available to all.

In the summer of 1887 Turner left the school to take up a position as headmaster of Dunheved

College and Thomas Jackson, who had previously taught at Kingswood School,[27] was appointed as his replacement. Under his headmastership the school witnessed '…the birth of a more vigorous public spirit, and the establishment of a higher standard of education throughout the school. E. Coleman, the first of the school's entrants to the London Matriculation exam, and ultimately to university, gained a first-class result. Previously 'unless a boy was destined for a university or professional career public examinations were not regarded as important'; the school entered boys for the College of Preceptors Examinations[28].

From the earliest point sport, especially team games, was enthusiastically played; it provided a relief from the more strict academic aspect of

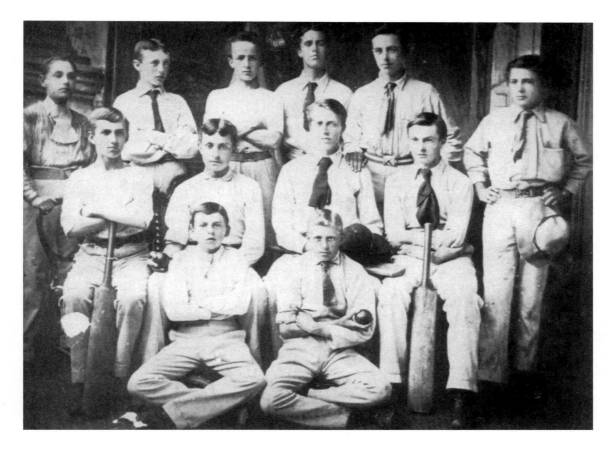

The 1883 school cricket team: H. Wills, H. Chenhalls, H. Boyns, W. Mitchell, W. Smith, O. Johnson, H. Jenkin, E. Boyns, R. Boyns, C. Richards, H. Hawken, H. Martyn

school life. The early team photographs show teams made up of boys and masters – which suggests some of the teachers were not as distant and remote as they might have appeared. At first a field up the hill from the school, near the Lander Monument, was used for football practice. During the early 1880s 'football was enthusiastically played under the rugby rules. We had a capital team and it was the exception to be beaten, even though many of our opponents were men of no mean size or strength'[29]. This suggests there was a lack of school teams to play.

By 1887 football was in a transition stage from rugby to association: 'football at this time was very much in need of an enthusiastic supporter... the new game had no slight struggle to oust the old from the field, and for some time the two were played on alternate days'. It was not until Mr Brown, a keen rugby enthusiast and county player, left that soccer became the regulation game. The first soccer match was played against Falmouth, and the result 'though an accident, was two goals to one in our favour'. However it took a long time 'before the team learnt to discard the mere brute force that had characterised their rugby play and adopted the science of the new game'[30]. Ernest Coleman, a former pupil, recalled his time at Truro College in the late 1880s, writing from Guy's Hospital '...though I was in the 1st XV for about three years, and played in nearly all the matches, yet I do not remember playing in one which we won. Though I must confess I sigh when I remember that the School has forsaken rugby, in which game it was once the first school in Cornwall, yet I am glad to

An advert for the school in 1888, with adverts for the Methodist Girls' Schools in Penzance and Camborne

find that the new game is played with such marked success'[31].

The school from an early time had a 'fairly good' cricket team though generally Cornwall was seen as disadvantaged in its facilities for developing cricketers. Initially a field near the railway 'not withstanding hillocks innumerable and grass luxuriant, gave scope for learning the mysteries of cricket'[32]. Then in 1886 the school acquired the former county cricket ground on St Clement's Hill for its sporting uses. Not long after a cricket pavilion was built on the new pitch because 'it was by no means pleasant to keep the cricket things in a cow-house and to be without shelter in the field'[33]. The money used for this purpose was initially intended for athletics, but the latter had procured little interest. The 'Sports Fund' was `aided by Mr Taylor, one of the teachers, who gave Shakespearian

Recitals[34]. Despite the new facilities, there was little success in cricket but in 1889 all the 1st XI won all their matches.

The racquet court, built in 1884, 'had long lain idle', but Mr Jackson, 'an expert in the game' set about reviving it. Jackson was also enthusiastic for tennis, and a hard court was laid in the upper playground and grass court on the field[35].

The Debating Society provided another activity outside of school hours. The earliest recorded meeting was on 21 February 1884 when the topic discussed was the success of the government and its policies. There was a majority of nine votes in favour of Mr Gladstone's government, and the result was communicated to the Prime Minister. They received a reply from a parliamentary aide, "I am directed by Mr Gladstone to inform you that he has received the communication which you have

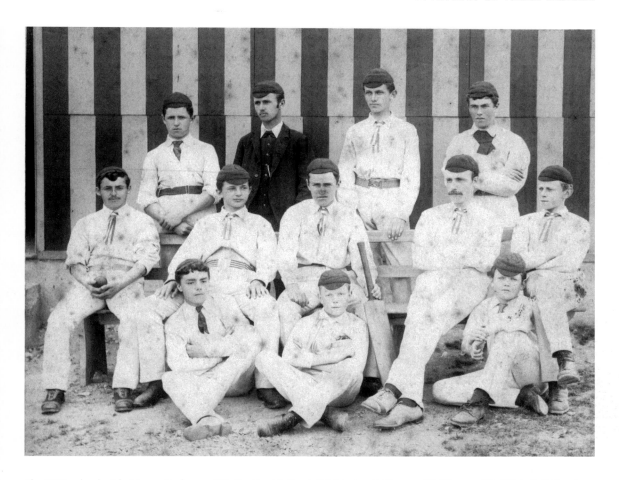

The 1886 school cricket team. Back row: H.C. Hockin, J.B. Read, T.G. Martyn, E. Thomas. Middle row: T.R. Mitchell, F. Geach, E. Vine, Mr Vinter (at that time fifth form master and deputy head), A. Holman. Front row: H. Boyns, E. Hosking (died in the Boer War), M. Lowry

done him the honour to send him, and to convey to you his thanks for the expression of approval and confidence in Her Majesty's Government which it contains"[36]. The debates proved to be popular with both boys and teachers alike.

During 1887, Jubilee celebrations for the Queen were held at the school. The college building was outlined with fairy lights and 800 candles were placed in all the windows, arranged to form the Cornish coat of arms. As a result 'the blaze was seen for miles around'[37].

Mr Glasspoole left at Christmas, 1888; he had been a music master who introduced a 'brazen age' into the school. He enthusiastically taught all manner of brass instruments but the resulting band showed little success. His temporary successor was a Mr 'X' 'whose short stay here was an unending source of amusement to all. It would be hard to say what instrument he excelled in …He habitually carried with him many potent drugs, perhaps to soothe his troubled conscience. His conversations had many references to Maharajas and other eastern potentates, whose Indian addresses he had by the score. He shewed us also a very elaborate duet for tambourine and piano…'[38].

During the 1880s the foundations of school life were laid, and a tone set, through newly emplaced customs that would create the school's traditions, that would enable the school to continue to grow and develop.

School photograph from c.1888. Thomas Jackson, headmaster 1887-1889 sits in the centre with H.W. Vinter on his right

The First Pupils Admitted in January 1880

J. Arthur, Sidney Bazeley, E. Boyns, R.S. Boyns, Howard Chenhalls, J. Furniss, F.J. Hart, Harvey Hodge, Jenkin, J.A. Jennings, Tom Jennings, F. Jose, R. Lewis, Samuel Lewis, H. Lord, T.M. Lowry, F.W. McCoskrie, H. Mitchell, William Mitchell, F.J. Nettle, William Olds, B. Paul, Herbert Paul, J. Paul, George Penleric, Joseph Prisk, John Richards, M.P. Richards, H. Thorne, Bernard Trehair, A. Trounson, A. Walters, Robert Henry White, Edward H. Wilton, T. Wilton.

The Curriculum in the Late 19th Century and Late 20th Century

1880s

The school aimed to provide 'a thorough English education … obtained at a moderate cost'.

The course of study was made up of:

'I.   Scripture

II.   The English Language in all its Branches, (Special attention being paid to Reading Aloud, Writing and Composition).

III.   History and Geography.

IV.   Arithmetic (Special – including Mental), Book-keeping and Mensuration, Algebra, Geometry, Trigonometry etc.

V.   Elementary Sciences.

VI.   Freehand Drawing.

VII.   Languages (Latin, German and French).

Extras – Greek, Advanced Drawing, Shorthand, Music and Practical Chemistry.'

1990s

Courses studied at A-level and G.C.S.E. include Ancient History, Art, Biology, Business Studies, Chemistry, Chinese, Design, Economics, English, English Literature, French, Geography, Geology, German, History, History of Art, Maths, Further Maths, Music, Latin, Physics, Physical Education, Politics, Portuguese, Religious Education, Spanish, Theatre Studies.

Pupil Numbers 1880 – 1918					
1880	35	1894	109		
1882	120	1896	100	1908	135
1884	132	1898	129	1910	135
1886	105	1900	117	1912	132
1888	107	1902	93	1914	143
1890	102	1904	94	1916	139
1892	94	1906	119	1918	166

George Owen Turner, the first headmaster
(copyright rcm TEsch152)

G.O. Turner (1880-1887)

George Turner was appointed the first headmaster of Truro College in 1879. Born in Southampton, he had previously taught as an assistant master, at Dunheved College, Launceston. At the commencement of the school he was one of two teachers and was directly involved in teaching the pupils. He was frequently described as one of the main pioneers of the school; 'during these years Mr Turner did much to lay the foundations for future success, and many of the best traditions of the school date back to his time. Others have entered into his splendid pioneer work and are profoundly thankful for the high ideals, which inspired his life and work'[1]. He oversaw the move of Truro College from Strangways Terrace, River Street and Lemon Street to newly built premises in 1882.

Turner lived initially at the school in Strangways Terrace with his wife, Mary and two daughters, Lillian and Ethel, and a number of the boarders. When the school moved into the new building on the edge of Truro, he took up residence with his family in the headmaster's apartments. His family expanded while they were in Truro when a son was born in the mid 1880s.

In the summer of 1887 Turner left Truro with his family, to return to Dunheved College as headmaster. A cricket match between past and present pupils, with a celebratory tea was held as a leaving party. Among the many tributes given to Mr and Mrs Turner the 'allusion to the motherly care of Mrs Turner elicited from the younger scholars a hearty cheer, which was the most eloquent tribute Mrs Turner could receive'. It was also affirmed that though the directors put up the building, '...Mr Turner had made the school' with the help of his wife. In recognition for their work they were presented with a walnut Davenport and a large glass salad bowl with silver mountings[2].

Before long he moved to Edinburgh, where he ran a private school. His final years were spent, with his now invalided wife, in Birmingham, where his son was engaged in teaching. During the First World War he 'got into the harness again' and taught for almost three years in King Edward's Grammar School. For the last two years he devoted his time to private coaching and work in the Methodist Church[3]. He died in September 1921, aged 72.

Despite moving away from Cornwall Turner continued his interest in Truro College; he was made a patron of the Old Boys' Association when it was formed in 1895 and returned in the summer of 1903 to preside at the College's speech day. It was through his connections to Truro College and Dunheved that an annual football match was set up between the two colleges. In addition a scholarship was founded allowing a pupil from Truro College a teacher training position at Dunheved.

At several early old boys' gatherings fond memories were recalled of the school under Turner and his wife. F.W. McCoskrie, the first head prefect, recalled that 'the education was given in a first-class way by Mr Turner... It was pleasantly and effectively administered... in a manner leaving little or nothing to be desired. There was one great feature in the school life – the motherliness of Mrs Turner ... that made the school after all a home'[4]. It is unclear how much of this was softened by time, but many others noted similar memories.

Thomas Jackson, the second headmaster

T. Jackson (1887-1889)

Thomas Jackson succeeded George Turner as headmaster in 1887. He had previously been a student and master at Kingswood School, like several other teachers at Truro College, before he came to Truro. He was a keen sportsman, who was enthusiastic about football and racquet sports. Although there were no dramatic changes made to the school while he was headmaster there was an increased emphasis on improving exam results, which was marked by replacing outdated text books and the first university matriculation. It was also at this time that the school team sport officially changed from rugby to football, although it took time to displace old practices. 'His enthusiasm in school and in games, his graceful eloquence in the debating society, and his geniality at all times were the life of the school ...'[1].

After leaving Truro College, at Christmas 1889, Jackson left England to take up a position as headmaster of Wesley College in Auckland, New Zealand[2]. In 1906 Thomas Jackson was compelled to resign his position as headmaster of Prince Albert College, Auckland, due to serious illness. He had been headmaster there for the past 11 years. When he returned to England he lived in Romford[3], before taking up a teaching post in Portsmouth. Jackson eventually retired from his position as Head of the Arts Department of the Municipal College, Portsmouth, in July 1924[4].

Like Turner, Jackson remained in contact with Truro College. With Turner he was patron of the Old Boys' Association when it was first begun. In the July 1930 issue of the school magazine he wrote an article for the 50th anniversary of the school's foundation. He remembered many aspects of school life including the College bookseller, Mr Clyma, who was no longer in the town.

After his death in October 1933 he was remembered in the school magazine. 'In his last years of retirement, bodily strength decayed, but there was no abatement of mental power', and he would be remembered for his 'sterling character' and his 'kindness… and unbounded enthusiasm'. While at the school, for two years, he 'did much to create a more vigorous public spirit and to establish a higher standard of education throughout the school'. Discipline during school hours was thought to be more rigid than before. He introduced the 'permit' system that extended liberties and encouraged independence of the school at all times. It was also added that 'some of the old boys did not know what his iron rule had been, but they did appreciate what Mr Jackson did for them'[5]. He was very active in school sports, and had a 'strong personality' encouraging many at the school to have 'admiration for his fine scholarship and sincerity of heart'[6].

The School Grace

Benedic, Domine, nobis et scholae nostrae quam ad Majorem Tuam Gloriam curamus constituendam per Jesum Christum Dominum Nostrum.

1890-1899

1890 – 1899:
The School and the Wider World

Just before the Christmas concert, at the end of the autumn term 1889, Thomas Jackson announced his imminent departure from the school, to take up an appointment in New Zealand. Herbert Vinter, who had been second master at the school, took up the headmastership in Jackson's place the following term, in January 1890. It was viewed as unconventional to promote a second master in the school he was already in, but because of the short space of time between the autumn and spring terms, with the Christmas festivities, and because it was only half way through the school year, Vinter was the best and most available candidate. Under Vinter the school progressed in a similar vein as before. Sport continued to flourish and new buildings and equipment led to the rising popularity of new subjects such as physics and chemistry; 'there was no difficulty in getting the boys to learn certain subjects, such as science, but there was still a lack of enthusiasm in Latin'[1]. Under Vinter's long tenure as headmaster the school witnessed many changes within itself and in the wider world.

Truro College was quickly gaining connections with other Methodist founded schools, including Kingswood School, near Bath. In 1895 Thomas G. Osborn, the former headmaster of Kingswood School presented the prizes at Speech Day. Osborn spoke of his relationship to the school in Truro. 'He was one of the committee who first broached the idea of the college. He was connected with it in its earliest days, and was one of the earliest shareholders in it. He had always felt a great interest in its progress and in its success …'. Osborn concluded with the belief that Truro College was successfully striving for better academic results and was unlike public schools that turned out nothing but professional cricketers or footballers[2]. Several of the teachers at the College in the late nineteenth century had been pupils, or taught previously at Kingswood. These included the previous headmaster Thomas Jackson, who was accompanied from Kingswood by George H. Hunter, and slightly later

Ernest G. Gane, 'one of Osborn's protégés' was appointed second master[3].

Like every era there were a few teachers who left an imprint on the school. Several teachers played in the school football and cricket teams, including the headmaster. The characters of individual teachers helped to colour the school's overall approach and provided models for the pupils. Mr Gane was known for his '"…strong personality, his keen intellect, his abhorrence of humbug, his clear concept of justice [and] his devotion to duty", but he also had "a trait of remote shyness …[that made him] more respected than liked"'[4]. Mr Hunter was involved in many aspects of school life, especially sports, the debating society, editing the school magazine and was noted for his musical ability, particularly as a cellist. 'His personality was endowed with a degree of 'magnetism', which strongly attracted the respect of boys of all ages and his zeal for his work enabled him to exercise a wide influence over his pupils'[5].

In August 1895 the Old Boys' Association was established in an attempt to maintain the interest of former pupils in the school's prosperity. 'On the evening of the Speech Day of 1895 an enthusiastic meeting took place, and the nucleus of what I trust will prove a large and powerful association was formed'[6]. It would give opportunities for the school and old boys to assist each other, while encouraging present pupils to emulate the success of past pupils. By the end of the first year the total membership was 68 and included past and present masters[7]. It was not long before Truro College steadily increased its contacts around the world. In 1894 Gane left to be the first headmaster at the newly founded Kingswood College in South Africa – whose motto was also *esse quam videri*. Similarly Hunter left for Queenstown College in South Africa, in 1897, and was later joined by H. Wilkinson, who succeeded him as headmaster there. Mr Jackson spent several years in New Zealand and Australia, while other former Truro College teachers emigrated to wide reaches of the globe including Canada and China. It was not only teachers who emigrated or travelled. Several old boys emigrated from Britain pursuing their careers, such as mining in South Africa.

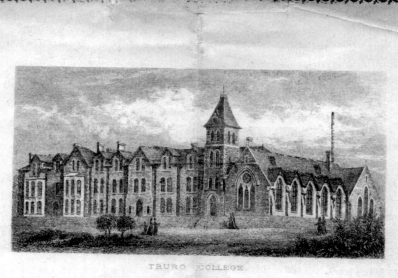

TRURO COLLEGE.

CORNWALL
Wesleyan Methodist School Association,
(LIMITED.)

✠ TRURO ✠ COLLEGE. ✠

DIRECTORS.

Chairman:
THE PRESIDENT OF THE WESLEYAN CONFERENCE.

Vice-Chairman:
W. BICKFORD-SMITH, ESQ., M.P., *Trevarno, Helston.*

REV. W. H THOMPSON,......*Truro.*	REV. G. MARRIS, ...*Truro.*
Chairman of the Cornwall District.	MR. ALFRED LANYON, C.C. ....*Redruth.*
MR. W. J. CLYMA, ...*Truro*	„ T. S. LOWRY, ...*Camborne.*
„ JOHN DOIDGE, ...*Truro.*	„ W. H. P. MARTIN, J.P..........*Truro.*
„ SAMUEL HICKS,...............*Newquay.*	„ W. RABLING, J.P................*Camborne.*
„ AMOS JENNINGS, J.P. ......*Truro.*	„ W. H. SOLOMON, J.P..........*Falmouth.*
„ JOHN LAKE, ...*Truro.*	„ H. T. WILLIAMS, ...*Redruth.*

Bankers:
THE DEVON & CORNWALL BANKING COMPANY, (LIMITED.)
Secretary:
MR. C. BRYANT, *Miners' Bank, Truro.*

A school prospectus from 1890

Before the Old Boys' Association was founded, sports matches were played between the old boys and present pupils. The earliest reference to the old boys' cricket match was in July 1891, won by the present team, which was then followed by an impromptu tennis tournament, won again by the present. By the following year it appeared that the old boys' day would become an annual fixture, with a cricket match and tennis contest[8]. It was not long before a football match was proposed. It had been difficult to set up an old boys match before this time because the school was changing from rugby to soccer rules. Consequently at the end of the autumn term in 1892 the first match took place under association rules or 'under any rules at all'[9].

In addition to the gatherings centred around sport by July 1897 annual meetings were also held and combined with a supper; a forerunner of the first annual dinner, which was held on 16 February 1905 at Princes Restaurant in Truro with about sixty guests present.

The school itself continued to change as new buildings were built to accommodate the growing number of pupils and the demand for improved facilities. During speech day in 1895 Vinter spoke of his desire to develop science at the school, which at the time was held up by lack of apparatus. By the end of the decade the first physics laboratory was built, and not long after the chemistry laboratory was also completed. The terraces in front of the main building continued to be cut out of the hill; another completed by late 1894 was used for net practice and tennis. It was not unusual for the boys to be involved in creating the new terraces[10]. In 1893 'Carn Brea' the donkey was introduced to keep the grass short on the front lawn. He was not known for his vocal talent or beauty, but one school wit remarked in the school magazine 'we beg to offer our sincerest welcome to the College Donkey, and to suggest the immediate formation of a Deer Park'[11]. The donkey became part of the school scenery until his death in 1896 when he was buried near the tennis court on the lower terrace, under a laurel bush.

Queen Victoria's Diamond Jubilee in 1897 was celebrated at the school with the production of

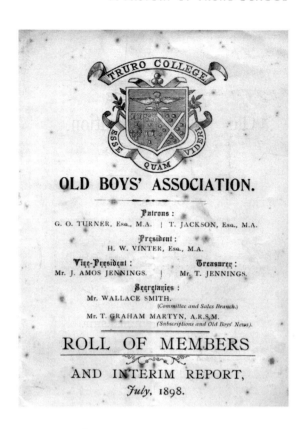

The patrons of the Old Boys' Association when it started in 1895 were former headmasters George Turner and Thomas Jackson. Herbert Vinter was President or Chairman of the Association until 1921

collecting cards, the money from which provided a flag for the school, and some money towards the new gym. A flagstaff, to hang the newly bought flag, was given by Sir George Smith of Treliske as his contribution to the Jubilee celebrations. That flagstaff fell down on Christmas Eve 1908, but was replaced with a new one made of Norwegian pitch pine. During the evening of 22 June, after the dedication of the new flag, the school was illuminated by more than one thousand fairy lights and from the school's high vantage point the boys and masters watched the many fireworks that were let off around Truro[12].

Half-holidays were given at the discretion of the headmaster and were annually given for the visit of the President of the Methodist Conference and for the headmaster's birthday on 26 March. Vinter established an annual picnic down the river towards Falmouth for prefects. Sir George Christopher recalled that senior boys were also invited to tea in the headmaster's study, 'I did not attain the seniority to justify invitations to tea in the august precincts. The evidence (never reliable) of lads who were so honoured, did not lead one to hanker after what would appear to have been somewhat of an ordeal; probably as much to the hosts as to the guests'[13].

The annual Whit Monday trip to Perranporth continued with the whole school spending the day on the beach, bathing, playing rounders and picnicking. On one occasion an 'enterprising youth … carried home an astonished-looking seagull, as a trophy…' and it was not unusual for the journey back to school to be accompanied by 'the wildly-mingled strains of 'Clementine' and 'Rule Britannia" which would alarm the local inhabitants[14]. The weather was not always favourable, on several occasions it was either wet or very cold. When the weather was inclement a detour was often made for older boys to see other sights of interest, such as stopping at Gwennap Pit to hear the annual service[15]. A few years later half-term excursions to St Mawes were also arranged.

A variety of clubs and societies were set up during the 1890s – not all of them successful. In 1894 a musical society was established to organise concerts, though recitals had been given before. Pupils and teachers in addition to special guests were involved in recitals[16]. An ambulance class was started to teach first aid and from the mid 1890s there were annual missionary meetings, at which invited guests would speak on Methodist missionary life in other countries. In April 1897 a magic lantern was bought to provide entertainment on wet afternoons. The first show, held by Mr Hunter, was of slides of Pompeii and Rome. The literary club, set up in July 1899, was short lived, though there was a later attempt with a reading circle. During the 1895 summer term a 'field club' was started to foster interest in natural things around them, such as snakes, insects, fossils and archaeological finds. Its initial purpose was to supply 'some object of interest to those boys who, on half-holiday and other field days, instead of joining the games prefer to loaf in the pavilion or saunter round the field with hands in their pockets, and their looks not always exemplifying the truth of *dolce far niente* theory.' It was hoped that the boys would become interested in the study and collection of outdoor objects of natural interest such as birds' eggs and butterflies[17].

The first issue of the *Truro College Magazine* came out in July 1891. Previously there had been a fortnightly newsletter, the *E.Q.V.*, named after the school motto, published under the editorship of Mr Hunter. 'Naturally the tone of this organ was not so elevated as that of its more permanent successor, and perhaps the nature of its contents may be considered as trivial'. By the time of its last days 'it reached a condition bordering on scurrility, owing to an animated discussion on Cornish nature', though it was remembered with some nostalgia and

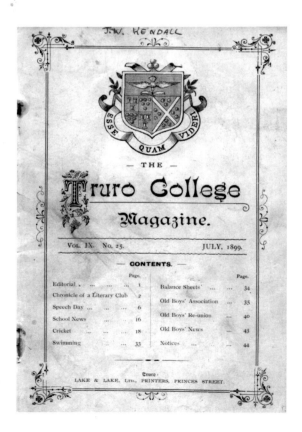

An early edition of the school magazine which was produced each term

affection[18]. It was later revived in 1896, but mainly as a schoolboy publication.

The main reason for the magazine's new form was to make the activities of the school and its news accessible to those interested. The new magazine came on the back of the success of a manuscript leaflet issued the previous term, which had attempted to fill the gap left by the E.Q.V. This had then led to a venture 'on a somewhat more ambitious attempt, and to present to our friends a regular record of the more important events in our school life'[19]. The magazine aimed to keep the old boys informed of the school's activities, maintain their interest in their old school and encourage school patriotism.

By the mid 1890s it was feared, as reflected in the magazine, that too much of school life was dominated by sport. In the December 1894 issue the editor mused that 'when the school magazine of the Millennium appears, we venture to predict that school games will occupy all its pages, and that an Editorial will be considered unnecessary and obsolete'[20].

Cricket and football continued to be the most popular sports played. Mr Vinter was himself an enthusiastic cricketer and 'he was then in his very best form … [and] run getting was not an altogether unknown thing in the College Cricket'[21]. Mr Hunter and Mr Gane were also keen sportsmen. However cricket often appears to have 'languished', when matches were won due to the leniency of stronger clubs rather than due to real merit. It was occasionally mentioned that Truro College cricket was such that if the team were without a 'demon' bowler they would often lose the match.

The first athletics sports day was held in 1891 and in 1893 paper chases were introduced as 'a branch of athletics'. The gymnasium was built in 1898 enabling sport lessons inside but even before the indoor hall was built and equipped, gym was a

The first gymnasium, which was built in 1898. It was designed by F.W. McCoskrie, who had been the school's first head boy in 1880

School photograph from 1893. The teachers are (left to right) G.H. Hunter, H. Wilkinson, E.G. Gane, H.W. Vinter, H.L. Beer, J.F. Parkes, H.H. Roseveare

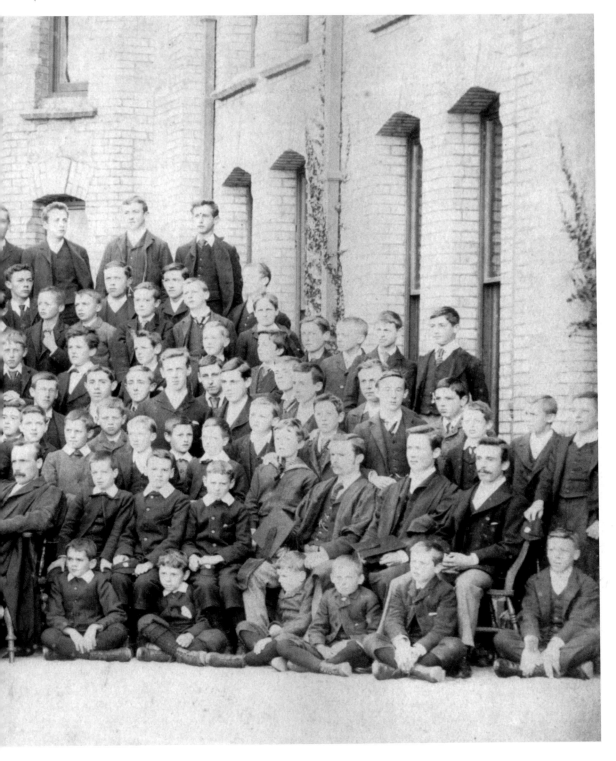

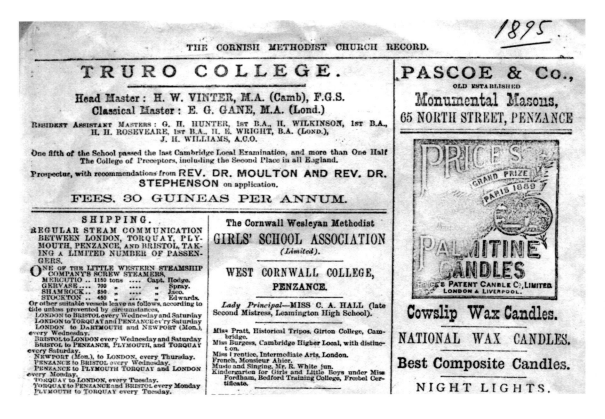

Advert for Truro College from the Cornish Methodist Church Record

part of the curriculum, although there appears to have been little enthusiasm to participate. The arrival of new equipment in 1891, the editor quipped '...seems to have aroused in a good many minds, the idea, previously dormant, that such things have another object than being merely ornamental'[22].

The opening of the Truro Public Baths led to the school forming a swimming club, which a large proportion of the pupils joined. Races and diving competitions were often held among the club and against local schools[23].

Football progressed under the coaching of Mr Roseveare; rugby was now totally abandoned. It appears that the association rules were new to many, including the teachers and it took a while before the College team was skilful. Mr Gane, like other masters who helped the football team, was a rugby player who with practice, had become proficient in the new game. Once again the school magazine

recorded the hardships of playing in winter. The writer complained that 'to change and trudge to the field, a process taking on the best calculations three quarters of an hour, does not seem worth while, with only twenty minute play in view at the other end. In a recent match part of the game was played in darkness...'[24].

More positive aspects to the game did emerge however and in 1892 the first football match was played against Dunheved College[25]. Soccer was becoming popular enough within the school for a football song to be written, and included in the school magazine.

In August 1894 a former pupil, Joseph A. Perry, who had been capped by the school, gave a shield for a football competition between the forms. The final for the shield that year was played between Forms VI and V, and won by the VI Form[26]. It later changed to a house competition when houses were introduced in 1904.

H.W. Vinter

From the 1890 Prospectus

Discipline was essentially made up of credit marks, with each pupil credited 20 per week. If the number of credits fell below 17 then permission was refused to leave the premises. Permits for walks and leaving the school grounds therefore depended on conduct marks.

Description: 'lofty school room (65ft x 25ft), five classrooms, dining hall (70ft x 26ft), dormitories, lavatories, sick room'. Outside there was a large playground, racquet and tennis court, covered shed for wet weather with gym appliances, cricket field with pavilion.

School rule: Boys must write home at least once a week

School hours:

Morning - 9.00 am to 12.30 pm with a break of 15 minutes.
Afternoon – 2.15 pm to 4.00 pm.
Evening Prep – 7.30 to 9.00
Wednesday and Saturday afternoons were half-holidays.

The school year was made up of three terms beginning approximately on 20 January, 1 May and 20 September. Six weeks were allowed for summer holidays and a month at Christmas.

Fees:

Boarders - 30 guineas per annum
Day Boys under 11 - 6 guineas per annum
Day Boys over 11 – 9 guineas per annum
2s 6d for stationery and books
2/- for the games fund, reading room and library
Drilling at extra cost.

'Holders of 5 shares in the Company, or those Parents that have three sons in the school as Boarders, are entitled to a discount of 5 per cent on the ordinary school charges. No reduction can be made for weekly Boarders'.

Extra lessons.

Piano or Violin – 4 guineas per annum
Organ – 6 guineas per annum
Singing – 1 guinea per annum
Advanced Drawing and Painting – 4 guineas per annum
Greek – 3 guineas per annum
Practical Chemistry – 3 guineas per annum
Shorthand – 1 guinea per annum
Woodwork – 6/- per term

Outfit of resident pupils:
3 suits of clothes (dark for Sundays)
3 flannel or 4 white shirts
3 night shirts
4 pairs of socks
3 towels (looped)
8 pocket handkerchiefs
3 pairs of boots and shoes
1 pair of strong slippers
6 collars
1 overcoat
1 umbrella
brush and comb (in bag)
dirty clothes bag
'College caps to be worn on Sundays and special occasions, play caps (with school crest) provided at the school and charged afterwards'.
Bible and hymn book
Small play box (not larger than 2ft x 1 1/2 ft x 1 1/2 ft) can be brought.

Herbert William Vinter, the third headmaster

H.W. Vinter (1890 – 1921)

Herbert William Vinter, the son of a Cambridge tailor, came to Truro College in the summer term of 1883 after graduating from Sidney College, Cambridge University[1].

Vinter took up the position of second master, at a time of expansion and further change for the school. He taught maths and science, and was very keen on cricket, often taking part in matches. He also '… made scornful comments about Rugger but very much approved of Soccer'. When Thomas Jackson left in December 1890, Vinter was appointed headmaster; Truro College was the only school he worked at for his whole career. He retired in 1921 at the age of 64, after 38 years at the College. After leaving the school he remained in Truro and maintained a close connection with the school. He was also a member of the Cornwall Education Committee from its formation and chairman of its Higher Education Sub-Committee, a Justice of the Peace, a trustee of St Mary's Methodist Church, Truro and a governor of Truro High School. He was also a keen supporter of cricket in the county. When he died on 19 October 1942, a memorial

fund was set up which provided a memorial tablet and the Vinter Room in the library (now part of the staff room), which was opened in 1950.

Former pupils recalled that Vinter was 'a man of sterling character, of firm but by no means unkindly methods of discipline, and sound learning of an unassuming and perhaps old-fashioned quality' and he gave 'the impression that he was a good man, rather stiff, but …he was certainly very understanding'[2]. Archie Marshall suggested that

within the context of the time and the school which was then more strictly Methodist than it is today, he was I believe a great Headmaster, devoted to the school and the boys. He showed us the value of Christian virtues, and for that I shall always remain grateful to him

These were qualities which pupils felt reassuring when they faced the world outside the school, especially in the First World War. However his outlook on life might have felt slightly restricting for the boys under his care, '…he travelled along a straight and narrow path, and I would lay the emphasis on narrow. His view of the bible was fundamentalist. It was a sin for a boy to show any interest in girls. This went for the staff as well…'[3]. John Rosewarne felt that 'Mr Vinter was by nature shy and this made him awkward when handling public crises' and that he '…was terrified by the thought of having to deal with a man who might be brutal or rude'[4].

Both staff and boys knew Vinter, informally, as the 'Old Man'. In addition to cricket and football he encouraged swimming, and became a director of the local swimming baths.

Life was difficult for anyone not really interested in physical fitness. In fact we led a rather Spartan existence. His discipline was strict but just and, …I cannot ever recall a sense of injustice. His whole outlook would now be described as narrow yet as a C. of E. there was never any feeling of discrimination. One can only say that the boys of his era were and are the staunchest supporters of the school[5].

On Wednesday evenings Vinter held a Bible class in dining hall with voluntary attendance, but a large percentage went, and again on Sunday afternoons, though attendance was compulsory this time, and included readings and hymn singing; 'the organ or large harmonium, in my time played by Frank Gilpin, led the singing. He played very slowly and the singing was dirge-like…'[6].

During the holidays, boys whose parents were abroad might stay with Vinter and his sister at the school. Vinter's unmarried sister, Emily, came to the school after he became headmaster to help with administration work and give music and typing lessons[7]. She had a nickname of Flip, and was often remembered with mixed feeling. It was occasionally thought that she had too much influence over her brother, and was often blamed for unpopular decisions such as the confiscation of permits to town. However she was also remembered for being different from her brother:

she had warmth and a sense of fun. Her devotion to her brother showed through everything that she did. If permitted she would have wrapped him up in cotton wool, and I suspect that her brother at times found it overwhelming. But none had a more devoted slave. She too was cast in the same religious mould, and was equally … straightlaced. Girls who showed interest in any of the boys at the school incurred her severe displeasure[8].

Miss Vinter's strawberry teas were remembered with warmth[9]. Rosewarne suggested that Vinter showed his gratitude to her for her service and support in many ways that was most touching.

Mrs Opie

After the departure of Mrs Turner in 1887 the duties of matron, both the care of the boys and the running of the household was taken on by Miss Martin. When she left the position was taken up by Mrs Eastman, who was later followed by Emma Opie.

Mrs Opie or 'Mother Opie', the widow of W. James Opie, 'mothered the school as matron for many years. She had a cottage in Mingoose, St Agnes, and a few boys whose parents were abroad, notably the Gilpins, spent some of their holidays with her'. She 'presided over all the domestic departments; kitchens and feeding, dormitories, sick parade, sanatorium when in use, clothes and domestic staff … [and] was said to have one sovereign remedy for every kind of ailment – a cascara'[1].

During the First World War Mrs Opie oversaw the running of the household, coping with rationing and a slender budget. No cooking was allowed on Sundays, so food was warmed up; 'even with the most modern kitchen refinements of today it is still difficult to cook vegetables in milk and to serve them up appetisingly'.

Mrs Opie gained quite a collection of photographs of old boys in the services, frequently asking for copies to be sent to her[2]. She retired in 1921, after 27 years at the school and died only seven weeks later, at the age of 71. She was remembered for her 'domestic efficiency, motherly wisdom, unbounded good nature, wondrous sympathy, and the happiest knack of getting her own way'[3]. Many old boys attended her funeral, as well as 40 staff and boys from the school[4]. The Opie Memorial Shield, given by her daughter Mrs Charles Bowden, was presented during the old boys' and present pupils' cricket match in July 1923, as the prize to the winner of the house competition - the first was Smith House[5].

Mrs Opie's immediate successors included Miss Parry, who herself acted as matron at the school for 25 years, and gained the nickname of 'Queenie'. Miss Parry, over the years had 'acquired a real skill in estimating the degree of illness of her patients, and many a boy has been saved from severe sickness by her promptitude in diagnosis'[6].

During the Second World War, because of the shortage of staff, Mrs Magson oversaw the housekeeping and catering. In the 1950s the matron's duties were divided; the matron focused mainly on medical issues and was assisted by a registered nurse, while a separate housekeeper was employed for the daily running of the school.

1900-1909

1900 – 1909:
'High on the hill with the city below'

As the new century opened, school life continued with the backdrop of the Boer War in South Africa. The school was quite enjoying the 'almost monotonous regularity' of the spring term after the pressure of exams before Christmas[1]. School life was often 'a sobering experience' for boys compared to home life. However it seemed like a little world of its own, above the noise of the city, 'even the rattle of iron-tyred wheels on the cobble stones of its streets seemed not to jar any more than does the tick of an old kitchen clock'[2]. The school had an average of 120 pupils and about two thirds of these were boarders. The successes of the football team in 1900 made up for the 'somewhat disastrous cricket season'; the cricket team having suffered from the loss of Mr Vinter, who was ruled out for the whole season after breaking a bone in his forearm while practising for Mafeking Day[3].

The war in South Africa was a continual talking point in school life at this time.

Among us, as everywhere else, foreign events have … claimed almost undivided attention, and every phase in the development of the South African drama has been followed with a healthy individual interest: patriotic sentiment probably never ran so high in the school. …Even in our small community, the experience of joys and sorrows shared by all has produced something of that feeling of kinship and fellowship which has sprung from the same causes on a wider scale throughout the Empire.

Several boys with family and friends in South Africa, had a personal interest in the situation; one boarder's mother was in Ladysmith, while his father was in Kimberley[4]. The success of the British in South Africa was widely celebrated back home and at the school with half-holidays. The relief of Mafeking in July 1900 was marked by the college with a half-holiday, fireworks and later there was singing outside Vinter's window in which 'sincerity and vigour compensated for the absence of harmony' before a march into town, along Boscawen Street with a banner on a broomstick and singing

patriotic songs[5]. Another half-holiday was given to let the boys witness the departure of the Cornish Volunteers from Truro.

While the relatively tranquil life of the school in Truro continued, several of the school's former pupils were participating abroad in South Africa in the war against the Boers. During the autumn of 1901 James Williams visited the school after nineteen years away, having spent the last eleven years in Murraysburg in the Cape. He was taken prisoner during the war and 'it was only at the intercession of his wife, who is a Boer lady, that he escaped more serious treatment'[6]. Letters were sent back from South Africa, and many were printed in the school magazines. Joe Thomas, who was at Truro College 1887-89, wrote to the school throughout the war, '…we have had no more fighting since the battle of Tugela, or rather Colenso, but have plenty of hard patrol work. One day last week we captured 500 head of cattle from the Boers; we exchanged shots, but nothing to speak of …'. The long hours in the saddle on patrols, the heat and conditions of camp were described in relative detail. Thomas also described skirmishes and battles, including Spion Kop. He had gone to South Africa with his brother Jack, and after the offensive met up with him:

Several hours afterwards when I was having breakfast Jack came up and said he had been too tired to walk to camp, so had slept on the veldt. He had had a very rough time, he was with twenty men (of ours) sent to line a ridge beyond our position, and he was one of only two who came out of it alright. We lost about 112 men and 2 officers. Old Price, who was a great friend of mine, and who was with Jack, got wounded, and I hear to-day he is dead. We are back across the Tugela in Buller's camp[7].

Both Joe and Jack Thomas were in Thorneycroft's Horse. Jack related some of his experiences at Ladysmith to the school magazine:

We, of Thorneycroft's, have not done much fighting this time; we had one or two engagements and crossed the Tugela first at Colenso, and held the position until the Infantry arrived; after that we did very little – held in reserve – until the day before the relief of Ladysmith,

Boer War memorial, originally hung in the school room but has long since moved to the chapel

when we, with all the mounted men under Lord Dundonald, made the last advance. That morning was the first time I have ridden over the field after a fight. I was one of four who went out in the morning to see where the Boers were. We rode across the place where the fight had been the day before, and it was something awful to look at, seeing the poor fellows lying dead and wounded, both Boer and Briton, and I was glad when we had passed the place. One doesn't mind that sort of thing when in action, but when one sees it afterwards it is awful[8].

Several former pupils had gone to South Africa before the war, either going home or looking for work, and were caught up in the war. L.E. Olver wrote from Grahamstown, where for six months he had been 'waiting for the war to come to an end' that the town guard had been called up to defend the town against the Boers, who are only 36 miles

away[9]. Frank Carstens wrote from Concordia, 'to say that he was Sergeant Major of the Town Guard at the siege of O'okiep, doing all the clerical work. From his narrative of the siege, we imagine he has had some rough experiences, and the relieving column under Col. Cooper must have been welcome'[10].

Not all the Old Boys who were caught up in the war were lucky enough to escape unharmed. Lieutenant Stanley Smith unveiled the school's memorial tablet, copper on a walnut shield, made by F.R. Pool, of the Cornish Hand-wrought Metal Company, in July 1902. The inscription reads:

W.L. Champion of Penznce, Nooitgedacht, Dec. 15th 1900.
G.E. Hosking of Pool, Vaal Kop, Oct. 24th 1901.
Martin Magor, of Truro, Elandsfontein, March 2nd 1901.

During the memorial service, in his speech, Wallace Smith stated '…the Old Boys who had fallen in South Africa were [not claimed to be] heroes of an ideal type, possessed of all the graces and virtues of which human nature was capable, but they did claim that they were true-hearted Englishmen, true sons of the Empire, who had given to the Country two of the most precious possessions that men had to give, their honour and their lives'[11]. Lieutenant Stanley Smith affirmed that many heroic deeds were not chronicled by the press. 'Champion was killed in an engagement in which he and many Cornishmen distinguished themselves. Magor died of enteric, and Hosking was killed whilst returning with a convoy … and a lonely cross on the veldt was the sole token of that heroic act'[12].

Martin Magor had served with the 1st Battalion of Railway Pioneers, in the 2nd Field Force[13], and like many on a military campaign died from disease and illness rather than as a result of conflict. George Ernest Hosking had been part of the cricket team while at school, and before the war started was in Johannesburg, before joining a local company stationed at De Aar, when the hostilities began. He later joined the 36th Company of the A.S.C. and after obtaining his discharge he was '…returning with his company to Head Quarters, when they were attacked by the Boers. The gun to which he was attached was in danger, and he and others, by a gallant effort succeeded in saving it. Hosking, however, was shot dead at the gun, and was buried with 23 others near the scene of action. His discharge paper was found after the action in his pocket'[14].

Champion was part of Major-General R.A.P. Clements' force the Boer force led by Smits and De la Rey. After attacking a convoy of supplies for the British capturing men and wagons, the Boers returned a week later to discover Clements encamped with his men in the gorge of Nooitgedacht. The ensuing clash occurred on the night of the 12 December and by dawn the heights had been lost and the British resorted to defending a key position called Yeomanry Hill. By the afternoon the British were able to withdraw towards Pretoria while their camp was being looted, 'having lost 74 men killed, 186 wounded, of whom 14 later died, and 368 captured or missing'[15]. It seems likely that Champion was among those who died from wounds after the day's conflict was over.

Back at the school, improvements on the first school inspection of 1904 had been made by 1909 and were quickly followed by more extensions and refurbishments to improve facilities further, including an art room to provide more space for students to work in. New examinations outside of the formal school qualifications were added to the curriculum; music exams from the Associated Board, Royal Academy of Music were introduced, as was the army qualifying examination for officer training. Unlike Dunheved and Radbrooke Colleges, which were also Methodist foundations, Truro College avoided being passed to the local authority following the 1902 Education Act[16]. The school's independence

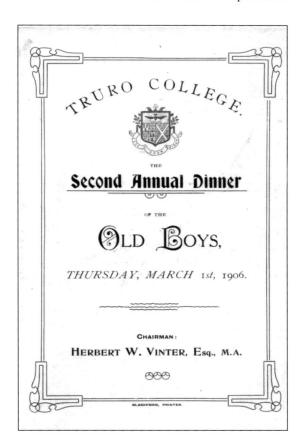

The first Old Boys' Dinner was held in March 1905

Inside the chemistry laboratory built in the early 1900s

was helped by the establishment of a county scholarship in 1903, which enabled a few more students from poorer backgrounds to have a secondary education in Truro.

To make sure that the school was effectively managed but without compromising its independent nature, the business aspect of the school changed in 1904; the company was liquidated and a board of governors was established in its place. When the school was set up in 1879 by the Cornwall Wesleyan Methodist School Association (Ltd), a small board of directors had been elected to oversee the management of the school, with William Bickford-Smith as the chairman. 'The College continued to be under the control of a

board of directors chosen by the body of shareholders until January 1904. Out of the Twentieth Century Fund a certain amount was allocated for secondary education and so the Wesleyan Conference was able to take the school over entirely at this date'[17]. Sir George Smith of Treliske, previously vice-chairman of the directors, was voted chairman of the first newly formed board of twelve governors who were: Mr Walter P. Workman, Reverend J. Reeves Brown, Reverend G.E. Young, Messrs W Bryant, W. J. Clyma and Hugh Rice of Truro, G.E. Stanley Smith of Treliske, James Wickett and Tom Wickett of Redruth and two members of the County Council. The aim was to ensure that all profit made would be used for

The school with the top terrace completed

strictly educational purposes. At the same time it was also recognised as a 'School B' by the Board of Education, a title to give others confidence in the school's equipment and work while allowing greater freedom in the curriculum provided and to be in a position to earn increased grants from the local authority[18].

In 1904 school houses were introduced, initially consisting of East, Hall, Tower and Town. Before this time school competitions were frequently won by either the sixth or fifth forms so the new houses were formed to make sport competitions fairer for younger pupils to participate in. However it was not long before the houses were renamed and house colours were introduced; red, blue, yellow and green for Tower, Hall, South and North respectively.

The College's 25th anniversary was celebrated

in 1905 and new classrooms, a reading room and a library were built to mark the occasion. Previously a classroom had been used as a reading room and part of the dining room for the library[19]. A physics laboratory was built in 1901, and later enlarged in 1903, when the chemistry laboratory was pulled down because its size was inadequate. When Vinter first came to the school in 1883 the chemistry apparatus was kept in a small cupboard in the schoolroom and there was one young enthusiast who was dubbed the 'doctor' among his fellow students. Six years later a small chemistry laboratory had been built. The new building in 1903 allowed more students to study practical as well as theoretical chemistry[20].

There was a dramatic fluctuation in numbers attending the school during this decade. In 1900 there was an average of 117 pupils at the school

The 1901 school football team. Back row: W.F. Brewer, N. Ridley, R.E. Rigg, T.L. Fiddick. Middle row: F.W. Burrow, Mr Fletcher, H.M. Nicholls (captain), Mr Fairweather, R.M. Kitto. Front row: T.H. Varcoe, H. Hancock

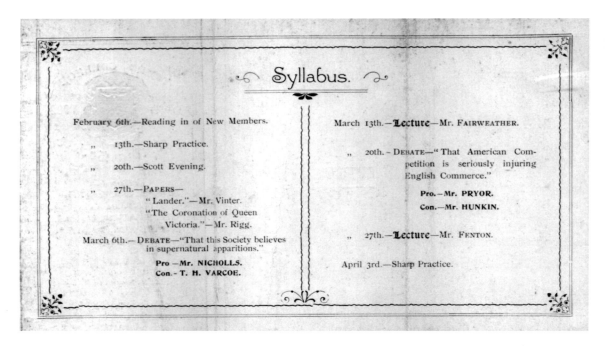

Syllabus.

February 6th.—Reading in of New Members.

     " 13th.—Sharp Practice.

     " 20th.—Scott Evening.

     " 27th.—PAPERS—
        "Lander."—Mr. Vinter.
        "The Coronation of Queen
         Victoria."—Mr. Rigg.

March 6th.—DEBATE—"That this Society believes
    in supernatural apparitions."
       Pro —Mr. NICHOLLS.
       Con.- T. H. VARCOE.

March 13th.—**Lecture**—Mr. FAIRWEATHER.

     " 20th.- DEBATE—"That American Com-
       petition is seriously injuring
       English Commerce."
       Pro.—Mr. PRYOR.
       Con.—Mr. HUNKIN.

     " 27th.—**Lecture**—Mr. FENTON.

April 3rd.—Sharp Practice.

Above - Syllabus of the Debating Society from the spring term of 1901

Below - The schoolroom in 1909

about two thirds of whom were boarders. By 1903 the average number attending was 90 and afterwards slowly rose again. Although there was a steady increase, which reached an average of 136 in 1910, the ratio of boarders to day boys altered considerably. By 1910 there were more day boys than boarders - a trend that would continue throughout the First World War. The previous highest number was an average of 132 boys in the school in 1897-8 and before that in 1884, but at that time boarders were still in the majority, especially four years after opening, when there were only 25 dayboys.

John Rosewarne recalled his first day at the school in 1909, which provides a vivid picture of the beginning of the school day.

The boys walked up the path, crossed the terrace and entered the school by the tower door or went around the corner of the school hall to the main playground. A small football affectionately known as the 'pimple' was provided. Just as I turned the corner I received my welcome to Truro College, an accidental one, a wet gravely pimple accidentally kicked full into my face …. The boys were called to assembly by a large handbell which normally stood on the long masters desk in the dais in the school hall. When the school was assembled the roll was called by the master on duty and the absentees noted. The Head then read a Prayer Book Collect…[21].

The school song, *Esse Quam Videri*, was sung for the first time on Prize Day in December 1909. It

---

Esse Quam Videri[23].

1. High on the hill with the city below,
Up in the sunshine we live.
Would you ascend to us
 listen and know,
This is a warning we give

Chorus:
When we are told "This is pure gold"
Let it be gold in its ring
Little we care what it may wear,
What is its self – that's the thing.

2. Come as our foe
 but by day not by night
Come as our friend, but be true.
Woe to the foe that's ashamed of the light;
Woe to the friend that is, too.

3. Shoulder to shoulder in war and peace,
Each of us sure of the rest;
Shoulder to shoulder, tho' hardships increase,
Never dismayed, or distressed

4. So we do duty in every man's sight,
Friendly to all save to spies;
Making no truce with whatever the light
Shows up-bolstered with lies.

By J.W. Hunkin (1899-1903)

---

was written by J.W. Hunkin, who had left the school only a few years previously, and was put to music by Reverend R.K. Vinter, the headmaster's brother. The school magazine reported that 'the music was spirited and well adapted for school voices, and the song was sung with great smartness by the choir, under Mr Thompson, the Music Master'[22].

The Reverend R.K. Vinter wrote to his brother, the headmaster, on hearing the song for the first time fifteen years later:

Those … words sung by 200 voices in perfect tune and with enthusiasm will haunt me for a long time. To hear the School Song by that volume of voices was a revelation of what can be made of even the simplest musical phrase hatched in the brain. In after years many an old boy will be helped to recall the school motto when perchance a few notes of the air rushes in upon him in a quiet moment[24].

By 1900 rugby was long forgotten. The school magazine featured an article describing how to play the game and comparing it to football, coming out in favour of football. Cricket was still played with enthusiasm and was the official sport for the summer. In 1903 a new cricket pitch was laid on the terrace below the school and to celebrate his birthday in 1910, Vinter was presented with a cricket shield by the school, which would be used for a house competition, especially as 'he regarded cricket as after all the best of English games'[25]. Tower were the first holders of the shield, led by their captain William Manners. The competition consisted of 'home' and 'away' matches being played over several days during the summer.

Clubs and societies continued and flourished, though many seemed to result from fads sweeping through the school. During the spring term of 1903 the newly arrived Mr Browning, who was enthusiastic about photography, urged for the formation of a camera club with its own dark room. A new musical society was formed in December 1904 when a 'wave of musical enthusiasm swept over the school' despite the music teacher having left. In 1909 the first of many chess and draughts clubs was set up among the boarders to while away the winter evenings, leading to in-house tournaments. The school magazine reported in the spring of 1910 that the school was in the middle of a new trend in pastimes; 'we have not escaped the epidemic of roller-skating, which may be indulged in … on every conceivable opportunity. We are bound to confess that several have attained a high degree of skill in the art, and serious spills have been surprisingly few'[26].

Letters from Former Pupils in South Africa at the time of the Boer War

'The war between Dr Jameson and the Boers gives us an idea who were the better marksmen. … We started boys to open up the mine, driving and sinking. Kafir labour was very plentiful, and we had about 350 boys on the property all interested in their work, but about the middle of July the news of the Matabele came, and the boys were very much frightened. In the mornings they would come to work with their blankets and assegais, and looking in the direction where they thought the Matabele would come from. I remember, as if it were only yesterday, when the herd-boy came in and said the Matabele were at Sapa Magoutea, an adjoining mine about three miles from our camp. In less than ten minutes all our boys, with the exception of our Cape-boys, had gone. We were about 15 white men on the property at this time, we all rushed for our rifles and ammunition, and stood on the top of a little kopje close to our dwelling house; but the Matabele did not come – much to our delight. The next day I rode into Victoria, 12 miles from our camp, to know what was going to happen as we could not get any news, but was told that it was time for us to leave the mine and come into Victoria. I left Victoria on the next afternoon, and rode through about two hundred Matebele warriors. They seemed harmless, as at that time it was not the white men they wanted, but the Mashona women and slaves. About two days after, a mounted messenger was sent out to tell us to come into Victoria, as they were expecting a big fight. We walked into Victoria, about twelve miles from our mine, in three hours, and over a very rough road, but no fight took place. We stayed in the forts for two nights, sleeping on the ground, the rain pouring down in torrents.

After the troops left for Matabeleland we went back to the mine. We had Cecil Rhodes and his party with us for two days, and a very lively time we had of it. The Battery Manager took our photograph. When the war scare broke out we built up the mouth of one of the tunnels (or drives), and took water and provisions into the mine, and slept in the mine for two nights. Two men would take a shift of six hours and watch the mouth of the tunnel, lest any of the Matabele should find out where we had gone, but they did not come. After the war was over, and the bones of Major Allen Wilson and his brave partners were collected, it was a sad sight to see some of the poor fellows' wives, when they found out that their husbands were killed. I went to the funeral at Zimbabye Ruins, and was very much touched to see some of the men crying. I must bring this part of my narrative to an end by wishing you all good-bye, as I am sailing for Matabeleland in a week's time'.

J.L. Morrish, April 1896

'Having refused an offer to go down country at the outbreak of the Matabele war, I decided on joining one of the troops which were being formed at the time in Bulawayo.

My choice lay with 'Pittrendrigh's Horse', a troop that had already done some good work. The troopers were mostly Africanders, but I am not one that will stick out because I cannot go with my own countrymen. Capt. Pittrendrigh was a most plucky and determined man, and was very keen on being 'up and at them', as the saying goes. I joined on a Saturday morning about the middle of April, 1896.

The following day being Sunday, I had no idea that we should be called on, so, as you may imagine, I was a little better dressed than usual. I was just a little surprised when I saw the troop marching down to the re-mount stables to get horses. I rushed off for my rifle and ammunition and joined the rest. We were drawn up in front of the Market Square, were inspected and marched off, 30 all told. Where we were going we had not the faintest idea, but we soon found out. After leaving Bulawayo, we were joined by Capt. Grey and 30 of his renowned scouts; this made things look a little btighter. We had not gone very much further when we met two of Grey's scouts returning with a prisoner; they had him tied to the saddles, and he looked very miserable. After a few moments' private conversation, the men were ordered to take him back to town; they had not gone far, however, when we heard two rifle shots, and shortly afterwards the men came riding back with the news that the prisoner had tried to escape and that they had had to shoot him. This was always a favourite excuse, all prisoners being shot early in the war. We had up to this time been moving very slowly, several of the scouts and our troop having been sent on ahead for the purpose of scouting. A messenger came back reporting that he had seen rebels close on us. We were ordered to canter and get within range.

I must here confess that with one exception this was my first attempt at riding. I did not mind the cantering in the least, but when one's horse starts jumping over bushes when you are not aware of it, you get thrown out of practice, only in my case I was very much thrown on the ground. At the end of the war I was a s good as the rest on horseback.

We soon found how close we were to the kaffirs by the enticing music of the bullets whistling above and around us. Orders were given to dismount, take cover and keep up a sharp fire; the firing was pretty stiff while it lasted on both sides, one man being killed on our side and one wounded; the rebel loss must have been about 50. a splendid opportunity was lost at this fight owing to the unfortunate jamming of a cartridge in the maxim gun, and our inability to extract it. One could not see many kaffirs to fire at, a puff of smoke from a bush being the usual target.

The scene of this fight was on the Umgosi river, about 4 miles from Bulawayo, the kaffirs were in large force and altogether too strong for such a small number as we were. One could not help admiring the cool way in which Mr Selous, who was with us, took matters. He was sitting on the ground calmly 'potting' at the niggers as if they were a lot of rabbits who had no idea whatever as to how they could return the fire. One of our troopers who was near him says he must have killed several that day.

I cannot agree with those young men who went home saying what fine fun it was 'potting at the niggers'. Probably had these same young men attended one of these picnics he might have a different tale to tell. If it was a matter of 'potting' them off one by one I would not mind, but it is the close proximity of their shots that makes one feel uncomfortable. When one hears the bullets whistling around in sounds of varying from the screech of an owl to the fizz of a squib, he begins to wish himself in the old home; and in my own case I would rather stand at the wickets and wait for a cricket ball than be a target for a ball of lead.'

R.G. Morrish, December 1897

1910-1919

1910 – 1919: 'Shoulder to shoulder in war and in peace'

The outbreak of the First World War in 1914 brought an end to the seemingly idyllic life at Truro College. Initially the school was little affected by the war, but it soon became apparent that school life was to be hindered or curtailed in several areas.

In 1910 the masters, as nicknamed by students, were 'Downey Mills, Hans Meyer, Taffy Ellis, John Lamb, Corney, Cube Orpet, Major Young, W.C.T. Smith, Bromo, Slickly Searle, Daddy Bunks, Sammy Atkinson, Messieurs Bleriot and Albert and the O.M.'. The 'Old Man' was the 'most respected and familiar of all'. Domestic affairs were run by the matron, 'Mother' Opie and Miss Cook, while 'in humbler spheres we miss Old Jim, purveyor of naval yarns of the very high seas, and Phillip Gill, shoe-black extraordinary'[1]. In the Speech Day report from 1914, Vinter reported an increase in numbers in the school with many boarders from overseas and

66 boys under the age of 14, and 'there was no difficulty in getting the boys to learn certain subjects, such as science, but there was still a lack of enthusiasm in Latin'[2].

The religious life of the school continued to be a major feature of the school week. On Sundays there was an hour of Scripture prep in the school hall before breakfast, which was shortened in the winter months, followed by prayers at 8am in the dining hall before a breakfast of boiled egg with bread and butter was served. This was followed by controlled prep or letter writing. John N. Rosewarne recalled that before going to Chapel on Sunday:

We collected our Sunday suits and white shorts from the workroom on Saturday evenings. Every boy wore a white boiled shirt with a loose starched front and cuffs and white starched collar. The Juniors wore Eton jackets with Eton collars but the Seniors ordinary lounge-type jackets and stand-up collars with rounded corners (square cornered collars did not reach England until

A school report from April 1910

about 1920). Every boy including the prefects wore a mortarboard to Chapel or Church. I think we must have worn black.

The boys marched to St Mary's Chapel in forms, divided in two and led by the senior boys, in the first division, through Boscawen St and into Kings Street. Before leaving school each division lined up against the wall of the school hall for inspection by Vinter, checking for any departure from orthodox dress. 'When cummerbunds – known to Mr Vinter as belly bands – enjoyed a brief popularity, one of the Spanish boys slipped through the net and to the horror of Mr Vinter who was sitting in his seat in the back row of the Chapel with his arm behind his back gave full display to the most magnificent 'belly band' that ever was.' Marching into town for the weekly service led to certain incidents when 'a number of young men used to find pleasure in standing on the very edge of the pavement outside Barclays Bank and leaning forward trying to upset the progress of the Senior division. The boys soon became alive to this and on the way to Chapel a hefty boy such as John Tregenza always took the left hand position in the front four. His job was to get his shoulder under any obstruction which might impede the progress.'

Once getting to St Mary's Chapel unscathed, the actual services varied in content. Fidgeting and any unruly behaviour was keenly looked for, reflected in the seating arrangements of the students. 'The junior boys occupied the seats on the minister's left, the master on duty sitting in the top row. The senior boys sat on the preacher's right, the prefects sitting in the two or three front rows. The school in my time took almost any boys who were offered and this created problems for some of the senior boys'. The boys' attitudes to the ministers would vary, and occasionally would be surprisingly in favour of those who teachers might not altogether approve of.

In those days, before the Methodist Union, the Superintendent Ministers were too high powered and perhaps too old to appeal to the boys. ...the second ministers tended to be younger men who were stimulating

thinkers. One who was very highly regarded was the Revd. Johnson. When the 1914-18 War broke out Johnson upset some of the members of the congregation of St Mary's by making Love the theme of his sermons. Being regarded by them as a pacifist they organised a petition for his removal. Pacifists are not popular with boys in war time but boys are quick to recognise a man who is on their side, one who comes to see their games and they have an unerring capacity to recognise and respect a man who is genuine. So Johnson earned and retained the respect of the school. One of my own cherished memories is of his cheery good night to us on a winter's night as we marched back to the school and he cycled past us on his way to his home in Probus...[3].

Boys at the school who were Church of England would attend one of the several parish churches in Truro, incumbents of which often had ties with the school. The 'church boys' were occasionally taken to St Clements by Mr Vinter. The Reverend W Graves, of St Clements, acted as an unofficial 'godfather' to boys from his native Isles of Scilly, and used to watch the school play cricket. In contrast St Paul's, which had leant towards the High Church practises, was not attended except on very wet days, because of its similarities to Catholicism. 'Church boys' usually went to Kenwyn, because the incumbent since 1883 was the Right Reverend John Rundle Cornish, Archdeacon of Cornwall and Suffragan Bishop of St Germans, who had been a fellow of Vinter's college (Sidney Sussex, Cambridge) and a master of English. 'The church boys occupied a few seats in the south transept but from the outbreak of the 1914-18 war the numbers began to grow and eventually they occupied the whole of the transept. The church boys were always accompanied by a master and occasionally by Mr Vinter himself'[4].

Patriotic fervour swept through school during the autumn of 1914 and many older boys and staff felt compelled to join up. At Speech Day in December 1914, Sir George Smith addressed the school, focusing on the prospects of the pupils:

The boys before him were living in some of the greatest, most formative, and historic times the world

The Cadet Band in 1915. The band included A.C. Rowe (in charge), Parry, Bradbeer and Bolton on side drums, C.F. Roberts and Glasson on bass drum, Keast on cymbals, Dyer, Boutwood, Hoskin, Thomas, H. Trewin, L. Woodley, F.K. Exell and Pearce on bugles. Mr Stringer sits in the centre

had ever known, and that the history ... being made .... was one of the greatest factors in their education for better or for worse.... He wanted the moral of the conflict to sink into the boy's minds, and make it part of their education, as they saw the great moving picture of every day's news – to know that they lived not for themselves, but for others, to learn willingness to sacrifice for public good, to put in their thoughts and imagination their country, second only to God[5].

Early on in the war the school was requested to provide part of the school buildings for Red Cross Hospital purposes if the need arose, though this was never acted upon[6]. Boys were often now compelled to finish their school careers early to help with a family business, as more and more adults were called up for service. Pupils were also encouraged to collect clothing and small luxuries for the war relief

fund, which sent parcels to France and the Dardanelles and money was collected for the Red Cross. In September 1918 on the suggestion of the Headmaster, it was decided that Olaf Odberg, one of the Belgian refugees in Truro maintained by St Mary's Church and its congregation, would attend Truro College for free[7]. Odberg was the son of a deceased Belgian frame maker, and stayed at the school until March 1919.

Several masters were called up, or enlisted. The headmaster tried to appeal against call-ups when the lack of teachers became quite extreme, but with little luck. Consequently women were first officially employed as teachers at the school; teaching the younger forms or subjects like music and French. Pauline Julian took up a position on the staff in December 1915, as a non-resident teacher[8]. The Governors displayed an ambivalent attitude towards

49

Truro College Cadet Corps, 'B' Company of the Duke of Cornwall's Light Infantry Cadet Battalion

teachers getting married at this time – previously all masters were single, or left when got married, because there were no facilities available at the school for resident married teachers. When Frank Dawson informed the Governors that he was getting married 'it was decided that in view of the present unusual conditions the matter was to be left in the hands of the Headmaster for the time' due to the 'great difficulty in staffing the school'[9]. Dawson left in 1916 to enlist, becoming an acting bombardier in the Cornwall Royal Garrison Artillery stationed at Pendennis Castle.

Different aspects of the war, its purpose and viability, were discussed in the school, often in the debating society. Topics ranged from the international to the local, with titles such as 'Should the War be conducted on more humanitarian principles?', 'Will Germany use her air fleet to bombard London?', and 'Was the U.S.A. right in giving coal to German warships?' The motion 'That compulsory military service is advisable' was carried by 10 votes to 6, while 'The present war was premeditated by Germany' was won 12-7, and the suggestion 'That the government should control the food supplies in war time' was resolutely won by 14 votes to 4. The students were therefore taking an interest in the reasons for war, and the various aspects of it. The debating society received a talk on travels through France near the Front and there were also some lighter topics such as 'Should Paris fashions be worn in war-time?'[10].

The Cadet Corps was established in May 1915, and was quickly very popular throughout the school; gaining the nickname of 'Caesar's legion'. It was initially established for older boys to prepare for entering the Woolwich Military Academy, though it was soon widened to include younger boys as well. Colour Sergeant Thompson, previously of the Dorset Regiment, was employed as the drill instructor and the first drill took place on 7 May, with 94 cadets on parade. This number soon increased to 97, with 89 boys and 8 masters taking

Truro College cadets marching up Lemon Street in Truro. Cadet Captain Vinter marches in the middle with Cadet Lieutenant Stringer. (Copyright Royal Cornwall Museum TEsch137)

part. Khaki uniforms were bought from Messrs Hobson of Tooley Street, London Bridge, which consisted of tunic, breeches, puttees, cap, belt and haversack. The kit was stored in a large cupboard in the gym, while it was proposed that an armoury would be built at the back of the workshop. Parades were planned to take place twice a week during term time, taking place instead of the cancelled cricket matches on Wednesday afternoons and after school on Fridays. The parades included an inspection of musketry and the use of a firing range by the V.T.C.[11].

Among the competitions that the corps took part in was the Wellington Cup, for the best section of cadets. Major V.S. Bryant, an old boy, then at Wellington College, presented the Wellington Cup 'to stimulate keenness in the Cadet Corps'[12]. at its inaugural competition. It was between the different sections in the Corps and judged by two impartial officers, who marked each section on several aspects including marching and close order drill. Section

III was the first winner of the competition, under the command of Sergeant F.W.C. Toms. Again they were praised for their efforts, but told there was not enough 'swagger' in their marching, which was 'extraordinarily correct' but 'lifeless'[13]. The College also took part in the Lucas-Tooth Competition, an inspection of Cornish Cadet Troops, in connection with the Lucas-Tooth Grant, and the corps with the most points would win a grant of £10. Brigadier-General Porter inspected the Corps in their tests in 1916, the first year it was held, and gave high marks to the College for their efforts. Consequently they won the £10 prize, after gaining 87% of the possible marks[14]. The College won the Lucas-Tooth medal in four of the following five years.

The Corps band was established in the autumn of 1915, and by the summer of 1917 the band was fully established as a bugle band, with four side drums, one bass drum, eight bugles, three privately owned bugles, and a pair of cymbals. The first members of the band, in 1915, were A.C. Rowe (in

Vinter as Cadet Captain

and together they marched to Tehidy, through the cold, with the band playing in front[16]. The Corps was inspected by Captain Tremayne of Carclew, and was praised for its company drill which 'is quite as good as that of trained soldiers, and does you all a great deal of credit'[17]. Mr Basset, the day's host, allowed the boys a tour of the house and various parts of the estate, guided by his steward Mr Everett. Before long it was time to march back to Redruth and as they did it began to snow. The smaller boys had some difficulty carrying their equipment, so older boys helped by carrying two rifles, one over each shoulder[18].

Teachers also took part in Cadet activities; Vinter was made Cadet Captain, while Greenfield became Cadet Lieutenant and Platoon Commander. After Mr Greenfield, Cadet Lieutenant, and Mr Chisholm, Cadet Corporal, had joined the Army proper their places were taken by Mr Stringer, who was promoted from sergeant to lieutenant, and Mr Wilson, promoted from cadet to second lieutenant. By spring 1916, Mr Dawson had also been promoted from lance corporal to sergeant and several of the older pupils were made N.C.O.s. On 1 July 1915 the Corps was officially recognised and affiliated to the 4th Duke of Cornwall's Light Infantry as B Company, which included a parade in front of convalescing soldiers who were 'pleased with the smartness of the cadets and the progress made'[19].

The *E.Q.V.* magazine was revived by April 1916; produced by an editorial team of L.P. Ingram, H.P. Bennett, H.W. Chegwidden, A.E. Tregea and A.P. Marshall, senior boys in the school. It provided school news with a dose of schoolboy humour. Adverts included a 'Laugh and Grow Fat Tonic – Guaranteed to make you smile in 7 seconds' and 'Infantry training – qualified instructor of fifty years experience. For terms etc apply Bennett. Kitchener Wants You!' The school news reported that 'we may now sleep in safety since Nish and Scotland have been on sentry duty guarding the College – Incidentally this serves to keep cadets in order' and 'we welcome to our ranks Mesdemoiselles Julian and Martyn. The mistresses go about things in a most master-ly way'. There was also a complaint

charge), Parry, Bradbeer, Bolton (sidedrums) C.F. Roberts and Glasson (bass drum), Keast (cymbals), and Dyer, Boutwood, Hoskin, Thomas, H. Trewin, L. Woodley, Exell and Pearce (bugles). It was probably at this time that the photograph of the band was taken. Their first public appearance was on 24 May at an inspection by Major Bain[15].

The cadets had marched from Truro to Old Kea, and back via Malpas, parading with rifles stored at the Town Hall, but the first major excursion as a unit was to Tehidy during the spring term of 1916. At 11am that day they marched down to the Town Hall to collect their carbines, before marching to the station to catch the train to Carn Brea. At 12 o'clock, when they arrived at Carn Brea, they were met by Redruth County School Cadets,

that April Fool's day had 'passed in dismal staleness, the only new joke being the keeping in of the school for ONE HOUR in the afternoon – for the point of the 'joke' consult the Head Master'. The sports news commiserated with fellow students that 'we are extremely sorry that the ancient game of marbles has not been indulged in so much this year. Perhaps the larger marbles have been commandeered for munitions...', while the Cadet Corps reported that each cadet was '... a fine agriculturalist. The 'calves' are in splendid condition thanks to 'forced marches'. The Drills at the shooting range are also numerous – Doubtless the Germans would be cow-ed if they saw us doing bayonet exercises in the drill-hall...'

In April 1918 an indignant editorial in the school magazine proclaimed that 'Mars is interfering with the larder' and that 'not only are the times out of joint, but so also the butchers, which is clearly absurd and indicates that the war is getting beyond a joke'[20]. There were 'serious' schoolboy complaints now that the war was affecting their stomachs, due to rationing. The wit of the editorial in the following issue reported that 'the list of casualties due to the rationing system is comparatively slight up to date; in fact, no really serious cases of starvation has been brought under our notice'[21].

Once the war broke out it was decided by the governors to carry on as normal, with the tenders for butter, meat and bread, which included Golden Vale Dairy and Thomas and Mutton, the butchers in Truro, to be left at discretion of the matron, Mrs Opie[22]. When rationing was introduced it was Mrs Opie who oversaw its implementation in the school, and she was able to procure an adequate supply of

The cover of the E.Q.V. magazine produced by students in 1916

good food. The food supply was slightly increased by the planting of potatoes by a newly formed agricultural society, who dug up the new tennis court and a nearby field for extra vegetables[23].

Life at the front and the war service of former teachers and pupils featured prominently in the school magazines, which were sent out to the various fronts as a reminder of life in Cornwall. Old boys, who often found it reassuring to hear of their former classmates, sent letters back to the school from the arenas of war. Although the letters were heavily censored it was still possible to get a sense of what life was like. The letters might include recollections of home and school life as Percy Philips' did in April 1916. He had transferred to the Royal Flying Corps, after enlisting in the Devon and Cornwall Light Infantry [D.C.L.I.], and was stationed in Mesopotamia, recovering from Malaria,

I used to pass on the Truro College Magazine to all the Old Boys in the Battalion. The copy I value most of all is the one dated July, 1915, which contained an account of Robert Gilpin. His death came as a great shock, and all who were at the College with him mourn for him as a brother. I had the good fortune to be in the Dormitory of which he was Prefect for several terms, and throughout all this time his influence was invariably for good, and I for one have never forgotten it, or his unswerving devotion to what he considered to be his duty. The four and a half years I spent at the College were years of complete happiness, and the lessons I learned there will follow me as long as I live. I shall remember all with the greatest possible affection and regard. I am very delighted to hear that you have started a Cadet Corps. The Germans may indeed tremble now, not because a Cadet Corps has been formed at T.C. merely,

Lt. Robert Gilpin, 63rd Battery, R.F.A., died on 3 July 1915 in Iraq

but because of the spirit it indicates. It shows that the boys are prepared, aye, and eager, to do their bit when the time comes, without being routed up by compulsion. I, too, am looking forward to the time when we can have a Grand Reunion of Old Boys, and though we shall miss certain faces, the predominating note will be one of gladness, and those who are present will be able to sing the Doxology with full hearts[24].

Other writers included some of the vivid images they had experienced as Alfred Chegwin, 2nd Lieutenant in 3rd D.C.L.I. did:

It is a starry night, but there is no rest. Overhead the shells of all types whine continuously, and incendiary shells and flares turn night into day. But this is nothing to what will be when the barrage comes down. Along the enemy line the number of flares increases as he becomes more uneasy as to our intentions.

With the dawn our uneasy barrage bursts like a thunderbolt, while 'SOS' signals flare up along his trenches. The scene baffles description. The air is thick with shells – ours and theirs – and machine-gun bullets scream overhead. We throw ourselves to cover as another salvo comes over and bursts with flash of flame and showers of earth. A stinging sensation in the side, but it is not a wound, merely a blow from a flying clod of earth. We

press forward. Already some prisoners are coming in, but the enemy is fighting hard. Victors and vanquished sleep their last close together in ghastly attitudes[25].

Letters also came from those who were prisoners of war or those who were laid up in hospital, as well as those active on the various fronts. There were tales of the mundane and the adventurous; Joseph Akester wrote of an account of an aeroplane chase he was in before being captured by the Germans, after going too far when observing enemy lines. Some letters also included references to more momentous occasions. A.P. Marshall, who had helped compile the E.Q.V. in 1916, was a paymaster midshipman onboard H.M.S. Barham, flagship of the 5th Battle Squadron in 1918, and witnessed the surrender of the German Fleet:

I myself happened to be look-out officer in the fore top and had the good fortune to sight and report the British light cruiser Cardiff leading the Germans, and the first battle cruiser, the Seydlitz, as they appeared through the morning haze…

Immediately on sighting, 'Action' was sounded, and we all repaired to our stations. That morning the Navy was taking no chances. Thus 95 per cent were deprived of seeing the whole meeting, for only about 5 per cent of a ship's company are above decks in action. About 9.30 we turned for home, forming two lines on either side of the enemy ships.

Thus we remained ready for emergencies for about three hours, and then we were permitted to come on deck to witness the whole review. It was a magnificent sight. First came five battle cruisers, which had three times joined battle with our battle cruisers, and each time had fled beaten, but still intact. Then came the battle ships, and following these, the light cruisers. The rear was made up of 49 destroyers.

So was the major and more modern part of the second finest fleet in the world being led slowly into captivity as it streamed at 10 knots between the avenue of British warships. It was a great and bloodless victory, the only one ever recorded in the naval annals of any power. It was the end of the German naval dream. For them the end was one of ignominy and shame. For us it was one of glorious and unparalleled success[26].

TO THE GLORY OF GOD AND IN MEMORY OF THOSE FROM THIS COLLEGE
WHO GAVE THEIR LIVES FOR THEIR COUNTRY 1914–1919.

G.B.BANFIELD	W.J.HILL	F.PENCELLY
E.C.BANFIELD	W.H.HOSKING	E.H.PRYOR
R.M.BELL	R.F.P.JACOBS	W.H.RICHARDS
W.BLAMEY	J.P.JAMES	W.C.RICHARDS
F.H.BREWER	E.J.JULIAN	N.C.RICKARD
H.J.BREWER	W.A.LAWRY	G.J.ROBERTS
P.CANN	J.D.LILLECRAPP	T.S.ROBERTS
C.E.COLLINS	E.LITTLE	H.A.SEYMOUR
R.C.CREWES	J.MARTIN	J.S.N.SHAFTO
T.C.CURTIS	M.E.MARTYN	R.D.SPARCO
L.DAVIES	W.C.H.MAWER	E.S.SPARCO
L.L.DREYER	H.A.MILLARD	F.B.STEVENS
G.M.FRIEND	S.E.MITCHELL	F.H.THOMAS
R.S.GILL	J.E.OXENBERRY	F.A.WALKEY
R.GILPIN	C.H.H.PARKIN	S.H.WHITFORD
J.C.GREGORY	H.M.PASCOE	N.C.WHITWORTH
F.L.HICKS	J.PAYNTER	F.WILLIAMS
W.FORD	H.M.NICHOLLS	C.R.RIDGILL

" THEIR NAME LIVETH FOR EVERMORE."

The First World War Memorial, now in the school chapel. The names are in alphabetical order except W. Ford and C.R. Ridgill, the news of whose death only reached the school after the memorial was unveiled in 1920

In response to the many letters from old boys, Vinter wrote hundreds of letters to servicemen, and John Rosewarne later recalled that 'several of my friends told me how good it was to receive, when involved in the degradations of war, a message from a man of great faith'[27]. Mrs Opie also wrote and requested photos, building up quite a collection of former pupils in uniform.

The war roll continually expanded and it was not long before a list of the former pupils who were killed in action was gathered. The war memorial tablet would eventually name 54 old boys who died in action. Lieutenant Gilpin was among the first of the old boys to die in action. He had been serving in Iraq with the Royal Artillery. It seems even more poignant because he sent back letters of his activities, and was the only one to have a photograph portrait in military uniform printed in the school magazine. Robert Gilpin died on 3 July 1915, after being wounded the previous day while

1912 Old Boys' Association Dinner menu – in a similar style to the April 1916 *E.Q.V.*

on reconnaissance work near the river Tigris, at Ezra's Tomb. In his last letter to the school, written on 14 June from Ezra's Tomb, he included 'I thought of May 1st, 1902, the day I joined Truro College. Funny how my mind went back to that day while sitting in the hot Persian Desert'[28].

Corporal Jabez Martin, with the 28th Canadian Regiment, died in a Leeds hospital on 1 October 1916, from infection after his leg was amputated, after he had been wounded near Courcelette, in France six days earlier. Lieutenant Charles E. Collins of the 24th R.F.A. was reported missing after the Ludendorff Offensive, which began on the 21 March 1918. He left the battery to go to the Observation Station, in front of the guns; when he arrived there he found the officer of that section had been wounded 'so he went down into a deep dug-out to see him and stayed with him a while. Another man at the guns said he saw him walking past … down into the valley which runs west from Lagricourt, and that was the last anyone saw of him'[29].

Casualties were not restricted to the army. P.B. Stevens, fleet paymaster, was aboard H.M.S. Vanguard, when its cordite spontaneously ignited at Scapa Flow, on the night of 9 July 1917[30]. Percy Cann was one of several soldiers who transferred to the newly formed Royal Flying Corps, gaining a commission, but was among the first fatalities after the R.A.F. was formed on 1 April 1918[31].

Not all old boys managed to go abroad; Geoffrey M. Friend returned from Australia to join the Veterinary Corps but was declared unfit for active service after suffering a severe illness eighteen months before. As a private in the Labour Corps he worked on a farm in Cornwall, to supply food. In the week before Christmas 1917 'he was taken very ill and was removed to the Nursing Home, Truro. He rapidly grew worse and passed away on Christmas Day at the age of 26. He and his sister were expected to spend Christmas Day at Truro College'. In a letter to the College at the beginning of December he wrote that 'personally I should have preferred to have gone to France and seen some of the fighting, but as you know, we have to go where we are sent, and must rest contented

Pupils Frank Penna, 'Chrissie' Cook and Frank Hocking with the schoolroom in the background c.1919

trying to produce food, as I expect we shall all be short before the winter is over[32].'

Tom Curtis was the youngest casualty, who, while serving in the R.A.F, caught influenza in the autumn of 1918, as did Harold Nicholls, who had been training on Salisbury Plain after returning from his home in Chile. However Truro College was little affected by the flu epidemic which was sweeping the country.

There were other old boys who became casualties of the war, though they do not appear on the war memorial. Arnold Varcoe of Roche, died on 5 September 1915 from wounds received in an August zeppelin raid on London. Herbert Whitburn had left a post in India to return to England and supervise construction work on behalf of the government at H.M. factory, Gretna. However the school magazine reported in April 1917 that he had recently passed away; 'his death was caused through overstrain owing to overwork, combined with the intense cold of the Northern climate'[33].

School war memorial pavilion, opened in 1920, with members of the football team and H.W. Vinter (copyright Royal Cornwall Museum TEsch023)

The school magazine of December 1918 declared that 'we are none of us going to be naughty and violent anymore', and continued its cheerful mood saying that Britain had been saved 'by her gallant soldiers and sailors, and has been handed over, for better or worse, to Mrs Pankhurst and the charlady'. On 11 November there had been vague rumours of peace during the morning, which were then confirmed by the headmaster at 12 o'clock, This news was met with much cheering, but the school's efforts 'paled into insignificance beside the din made by sirens and hooters in the town and on the river steamers'. The cadets changed into their uniforms, and by 12.30 they were marching into town, leading the rest of the school, to join the throng. 'The whole city was alive with people and gaily bedecked with flags'. The school marched around Boscawen Street before stopping before the town hall to sing the national anthem and 'Rule Britannia'. Then the official announcement of armistice was made and the day was made into a general holiday[34].

The lack of teaching staff was more noticeable after the war, especially as the number of students increased. It was not until there was a major overhaul of the staff in 1921 that the balance was restored. During the summer of 1919 an old boys' reunion was held for the first time since the war ended, and many survivors of the war returned to the college to meet up with friends and take part in the cricket match between past and present pupils. Gradually school life returned to how it had been before the war broke out; as exemplified in July 1920 when the school magazine proclaimed that 'King Cricket has once more made a triumphant entry upon the Field, for this is the first full cricket season we have had since 1911'[35].

By the end of 1920 the war memorial tablet and cricket pavilion were unveiled, to remember the former pupils who had died in the war. The pavilion was the fulfilment of a proposal from 1911, but its construction had been prevented by the start of the war. By 1918 however, a memorial fund was established and the headmaster had drafted a plan for the war memorial. It was estimated that £1000 would be needed to purchase the land on which to build the pavilion and to make the tablet; any money remaining would be used for school prizes or exhibitions[36]. The memorial tablet was unveiled on 5 December after speech day, by Major George Gilpin, brother of Robert Gilpin. Sir George Smith opened the pavilion on 8 October 1920.

From a letter by Flight Sub-Lieutenant J.C. Akester, R.N., Royal Navy Air Service

'On the morning of the 26th September [1917], the day of the big pushes at Ypres [the battle for Polygon Wood], I set off in a triplane (by myself) to do my little bit, and a very little bit it was, too. The sky was very cloudy, the clouds being about 2,000 feet high. I crossed the lines above the clouds, and coming down below the clouds I found myself rather too far over the lines, for there was a strong west wind blowing above which, of course, was against my getting back to our side quickly. After a little firing with my machine-gun at some German anti-aircraft batteries which did their best to bring me down, four German aeroplanes came down out of the clouds behind me. I turned round and started fighting them. After scrapping around for two or three minutes my machine-gun jammed. I cleared that jamb, when the blessed thing jammed again, and being unable to clear the second jamb I decided to escape if possible. I was under 2,000 feet high, and being five miles over the lines stood very little chance of escaping. The only thing for me to do was to dodge in and out of the clouds, shaking off my pursuers, if possible, and so worm my way back to our side. For almost half-an-hour the chase kept up, and my machine was riddled with bullets, but so far I was untouched. Anti-aircraft guns and machine guns were firing at me from the ground, too. At last I came to a big clear space in the sky through which I must go to reach our lines. The Germans put up a barrage of shells in front of me to prevent me from going straight ahead, but I managed to dodge them for a few minutes. Sometimes they would burst only a few yards in front of me, and one of them took a bit of my right wing away. But dodging anti-aircraft shells and the four aeroplanes, which were about 50 to 100 yards behind me all the time, was a bit too much for me at any rate. Finally I was hit in my left arm, and the bullet passed straight on and pierced my petrol tank. My cockpit was simply alive with bullets, and how I escaped being hit in at least a hundred places, goodness only knows. About two minutes later a bullet struck my engine and my revs dropped considerably, and therefore my speed.

I saw that at last I must come down on the German side of the lines, that which I had worked so hard to avoid. The ground was totally unsuitable for landing, so I ran into a whole heap of telegraph wires at over 100 miles an hour. I thought it would cut up their communications as well as smash up my machine for them. I don't remember anything after charging those wires until I was picking myself up off the ground (a ploughed field) and finding a crowd of Germans around me. I could not see my machine at all; goodness knows where it had landed. One thing, though, I was sure of, and that was that it must be smashed to atoms. Then I fainted; when I came round again my arm was bandaged, and a German Captain, the Commandant of Menin, was near me – a very nice fellow he was, too.

He took me in his motor-car to his house, and gave me some wine and pears, which he peeled for me. From there he took me to a hospital, where my arm was dressed again. I was then taken in a staff motor-car along with a German officer, who could speak English very well, to another place, where I had tea with some other German officers, and also another R.N.A.S. pilot whom I knew at Cranwell and who had been taken prisoner the day before. About 6 o'clock I was put in a Red Cross ambulance along side a number of German wounded en route for a hospital in Coutrai. In four or five hours we arrived at the hospital and before much longer I was in bed and fast asleep'.

In April 1919 after 15 months' captivity he arrived home and like many others took time to recover, though by December the school magazine reported that he was following a business career in London.

1912 Football Team
Back Row, Left - Right: H.A. Millard, G. Stratford, A.E. Tregea, G.K.B. Hay, C.E. Collins, C.M. Barnes
Front Row: G.W. Manners, T.J. Olver, W.J. Delbridge, G.R. Gilpin, F.E. Gilpin, H.C. Rickard, J.P. James

Truro College Old Boys in the First World War

Harold Austin Millard
b. 10.3.1896.
At Truro College 1910 – 1913.
1914 - private 5th Hampshire
Territorials.
1915 - Wessex Division, as a signaller in
the Royal Engineers.
d. 13 October 1915, aged 19. Corporal
186th Co, RE, killed in action in France,
during a gas attack, when, due to an
accident in apparatus, he was badly
gassed trying to save others from the
same fate. Buried Cambrin Churchyard.

Gerald Stratford
b. 18.2.1896.
At Truro College 1908-1913.
After leaving school went into
elementary school teaching.
1915 – 20th Service Battalion, RF.
1917, Spring – gazetted to 2nd
Lieutenant in 3rd Argyll and Sutherland

Highlanders (Regulars). Sent battlefield
'souvenirs' back to the College for
the museum.
1918 – wounded on April 8th, but
recovered.

Alfred Ernest Tregea
b. 3.10.1896.
At Truro College 1909 – 1915.
1916 – returned from Argentina with
his mother. Helped out the College
'assisting the Headmaster in the
discipline of the school'.
1917 – passed exam for entrance into
an Agricultural School in Argentina.

George Kingston Baron Hay
b. 3.9.1895.
At Truro College 1912 – 1913.
After leaving school took up farming in
Australia.
1915 – Private, Australian Light Horse.

1917 – Corporal, came from
Australia and now attached to 8/51st
Regiment, AIF.
1918 – Wounded in France in August.
Later awarded the Military Cross.

Charles Edwin Collins
b. 15.12.1895.
At Truro College 1906 – 1913.
1914 – OTC, Birmingham.
1915 – Passed entrance exam for Royal
Military Academy, Woolwich.
1918 – Lieutenant, 24th Bde Royal Field
Artillery, was reported missing in France
since March 21st. In the Queant Sector
when the battle opened, and was next
for duty at the Observation Station. He
left the battery position about 7am with
2 signallers; he had to go through a
section of forward guns to get to the
Observation Station. When he arrived
the Officer of the Section had been

wounded, so went down into the dug-out to see him and stayed with him awhile. He was later seen walking past the guns down into the valley, which ran west from Lagricourt, which was the last time he was seen. Thought to be a P.O.W. Reported killed in action on 21 March 1918. Named on Arras Memorial.

Cyril Maunder Barnes.
b. 10.5.1897.
At Truro College 1909 – 1914.
1915 – Private, RAMC.
1916 – Letter to the College: 'At the commencement of the 'Push' we had one lively day. Our total for the first twelve hours being just over twelve hundred. We did work hard for a day or so …I have met several O.B.s. The first one I met was Rowe, from Redruth, and the next was Chaplain Hunkin, and soon after I met King'.

John Pryor James
b. 14.2.1897.
At Truro College 1910 – 1912.
1916 – Private, Duke of Cornwall's Light Infantry, at Bovington Camp, Wool, Dorset. Went out to France in October.
d. 26 October 1916. Killed during first tour of duty in the trenches while on a listening post in a mine shaft.

Henry Cecil Rickard
b. 9.6.1897.
At Truro College 1909 – 1914.
After school went to Redruth Mining School.
1916 – 1/5th Seaforth Highlanders, added to school roll of honour.
1918 –Admitted to hospital in France suffering from exposure to gas. Returned to the Front, but badly gassed again and died 26 August 1918, aged 21. Buried at Ligny St Flochel British Cemetery

George Whichcote Manners
b.25.8.1897.
At Truro College 1912 – 1914.
1915 – 26th Service Battalion RF.
1916 – wounded in France, taken to a hospital in Birmingham. Wrote to the College, 18 May: I am in France and getting my share of excitement. We left England two or three weeks ago, and are at present close behind the firing line. At night we can see where the firing line is by the star shells and searchlights. During the last three days we have seen two or three German aeroplanes shelled. We are billeted in a barn, the floor of which is covered with straw. At night the place is overrun with rats, which go for our bread and cheese. We are not working very hard, and receive good food and plenty of it. We can even get eggs and coffee at the farmhouse. Papers are very hard to get. To-day I paid 3d. for an English paper a day old. I have come across one or two O.B.s and have had several long chats.
1917 – wounded near Gavrelle and Greenland Hill in May, taken to hospital in Sheffield.

Thomas James Olver
b. 9.8.1895.
At Truro College 1911 – 1912.
After leaving school worked in mining in South Africa
1916 – German East African Forces.

Frank Edward Gilpin
b. 29.8.1897.
At Truro College 1909 – 1915.
1915, March – passed the entrance exam to the Royal Military Academy, Woolwich.
1916 – 2nd Lieutenant RGA, stationed in France: As yet we have no casualties in this battery … Our infantry are splendid. Their courage, patience, and endurance are marvellous. I think they earn at least £1 a day each, and often a VC, but they get neither…They are cheerful and willing in the midst of constant danger…Now is a trying time for all, and the Hun is no fool to deal with – neither is our Staff for that matter. It is wonderful how coolly and smoothly everything works out. Everyone seems to be doing his best…

William John Delbridge
b. 23.1.1895.
At Truro College 1909 – 1912.
After leaving school took up an appointment with Messrs. Czarrikon & Co, sugar dealers in London.
1916 – d. 11 January, age 20 at St Mawes, after a long illness

George Ruddell Gilpin
b. 7.9.1895.
At Truro College 1908 – 1913.
Went to the Royal Military Academy after leaving school, for Royal Engineers.
1915 – 2nd Lieutenant, RE, Chatham. Left Anzac in safety when Gallipoli Peninsula was evacuated. Later stationed in Alexandria.
1916 – sent a 'phylactery' from Gallipoli containing parts of the Koran and a Turkish hand-grenade from Anzac to the school's museum. In the autumn he was stationed near the Suez and Port Tewfik, and recently on a reconnaissance expedition met RM Treloar (old boy), who was serving in an Indian battalion.
1918 – stationed at Ramlah. Later visited his brother Frank, while in India.
1919 – By this time gazetted Captain in the Royal Engineers, and was awarded the Military Cross for his service in Palestine.

1920-1929

School staff in 1928

1920 - 1929: 'A new era begins'

The year 1921 saw a dramatic change in the school: the closure of the Vinter era and the appointment of Magson as headmaster. This was principally marked by the arrival of a large number of new teaching staff and a similar departure of the old. There were eight new members of staff including the second master Edwin 'Bert' Willday, and the headmaster, Egbert Hockey Magson. Within two years the staff was completely changed from how it had been in 1918. Herbert Vinter retired at the end of the summer term 1921. On 16 August, the old boys presented him with a mahogany bookcase and bureau with a study chair. In response Vinter remarked:

If only I had the experience of the past thirty years, and began now, I could do much better than I did in the past. I owe a great deal, and I should like to mention it here, to Mr and Mrs Turner, when I came here first. If it had not been for the kind care of Mrs Turner I should not be standing before you this evening… My work is not quite finished, but I know my life's chief work is behind me … If I have had any success in this school it is because

I have been intensely interested in my work and have stuck to it…[1].

Vinter was praised for being 'the best friend Truro College ever had in its history', and it was commented that 'the biggest thing in life was personality, and Mr Vinter had held the whole of them by his winsome, tactful, gracious personality'[2]. On the same occasion Miss Vinter was presented with a suitcase and a breakfast service in appreciation for all her work at the school. Emma Opie, who was also retiring after 27 years as the school matron and housekeeper, was presented with a tapestry covered easy chair and because 'Truro College, under her influence, had been a home away from home, and as an appreciation of her heart of gold they gave her a golden present, with the best wishes of all old boys'[3].

The curriculum at Truro College at this time remained classical in style, though Latin never seemed very popular and the same emphasis was placed on science and sport as ever. The aim of the school remained to be a place 'where the soundest secular education shall be given along with the foundation principles of religion and the principles

Staff on the annual school outing, 1924
Top left – Mr 'Jimmy' Ault
Top right – Mr H.F. Marks and George Jervis
Bottom left – Mr 'Sammy' Way, music master

of morality; a school worthy of British traditions, where brisk and vigorous work would alternate with the moral education of the playing field'[4]. The standard of work had suffered during the war because of the lack of teachers and restrictions to facilities. By 1921 however, the sixth form, which had completely disappeared during the war, had been reconstituted, and consisted of 22 boys. It was usual for the Cambridge School Certificate exam to be taken in Form V because pupils were expected to matriculate to enter the sixth form. This approach was helped by independent study undertaken on Monday afternoons by boys in forms above IIIB, who were allowed to work on any subject in which they were behind, with help and advice from the teachers[5].

Top - Relaxing in the staff room between lessons, Miss
A.M. Warford, Mr A.C. Grove, Mr C.L. Ellis, Mr G.S. Elliot
Bottom – Three masters at the school in 1925

More than fifty percent of the students came
from London and the Midlands, reflecting the
school's increased appeal outside the county.
Magson was faced with the consequences of the
1918 Education Act, which raised the school leaving
age to 14, but also made class sizes much larger.
The content of what was taught varied, and
between schools there was often little coherence; 'at
a guess teachers inclined to the Right in the twenties and to the Left in the thirties…' and in addition
'the educators were left to decide things for
themselves. Anarchy prevailed, a last great bastion
of English freedom'[6]. In 1926 it was suggested that
the leaving age be raised to 15 and that there should
be a break between primary and secondary education at the age of 11. As a result the 'new system at
'eleven plus' increased the divergence between the
publicly maintained schools and the private schools

'En route for St Michael Penkevil', 1st Truro College Troop, October 1927

for the fee-paying minority where the break came at 13'[7]. At the College the divide, from the tuition fees at the time, was based on those under and those over 12. The average expected school life after the age of 12 rose from 2.4 years in 1913, to 3.2 years by 1924 and the majority of pupils were aged between 12 and 16, though additional measures were called for to ensure more 14 to 15 year olds remained at the school[8].

The local education authorities were providing grants to allow boys from less well off families to attend Truro College, especially those who lived in Truro, because the College was, at the time, the only secondary school for boys in the city. The school received grants in its capacity as a secondary school, which helped to maintain the Methodist ideal that education should be available to all. There was also a number of free places provided, averaging 20% of the total number of pupils. In fact, although there were tuition fees at the time,

they were deemed low in comparison with other fee-paying schools, and were often below the cost of instruction. This was because the school was dependant on the income from boarders' fees and it was feared that an increase in the number of day boys (because of the county council's keenness to provide more free places for local day boys) would lead to a fall in the number of boarders, which would change the nature of the school[9].

The pupils from abroad, who were still a significant proportion of the total student body, were sometimes called upon to help in Truro. In May 1925 Alfredo de Souza and Mario Pimenta, acted as interpreters for the Truro City Magistrates in a case prosecuting three stowaways who had been onboard the S.S. Elba (at that time lying in the Truro River) none of whom could speak English, only Portuguese. The stowaways were sentenced to fourteen days in prison before being sent back home. 'The interpreters did not desire any fee for their services, and they were thanked by the Bench'[10].

The tuck shop - 'that emporium whose stock favourably compares with the contents of a conjuror's hat, from whose depths the harassed vendors are able to produce everything to delight a schoolboy's eyes and palate...'[11]. - was still a prominent feature of everyday school life, with the profits going to the sports fund. It was jokingly considered essential training in the 'art of shop-keeping', and was 'an absolute essential to school life'[12]. Similarly in December 1929 it was reported that 'through the enterprise of the Tuckshop officials, wholesome hot chips are on sale on Saturday evenings; we are asked, however, to deny the rumour that champagne and oysters will shortly take a prominent place on our cuisine'[13].

1921 saw the loss of several old friends of Truro College. The first headmaster, George Turner died in September, while Mrs Opie passed away only ten weeks after her retirement in the summer. Sir George Smith of Treliske, a school director and chairman of the governors, died in October and not long after was followed by James Wickett, also a governor and who had sent all seven of his sons to the school. Consequently the school house system was changed as a tribute to the former governors: the new houses were Wickett, Smith, Vinter and School, each with a house master in charge and governed by a house committee of leading members. The change was thought necessary because 'the football and cricket matches were looked upon as duties rather than as pleasures, [and] because it followed as a matter of course that Tower House won'[14]. Points were awarded not only for the conventional sports of soccer and cricket but also for tennis, swimming, cadet corps, athletics and chess, so that any boy could be involved in the house competition. The Opie shield was introduced in 1923 as a prize for the house competition, and was first won by Smith House.

By October 1921 the Cadet Corps was reduced to three platoons due to the decrease in numbers, with one platoon consisting entirely of day-boys. The last mention of the Cadet Corps, in the school magazine was in December 1921[15] and it was disbanded not long after this. By the end of the decade

Top - May half-term camp at Hayle, 1928
Bottom - Truro College scouts past and present at the World Jamboree held at Arrow Park, 31 July to 13 August 1929

it had been replaced at the school by the Boy Scout movement. The meeting of the 1st Truro College Troop took place on 7 October 1927 in one half of Lobb's carpentry hut in the top playground, and was attended by nine boys and the scout-master, R. P. Ayres. It was established in response to a general feeling that public schoolboys were not becoming scout-masters on leaving school, which then led to the formation of troops in more than fifty schools, including Truro College[16]. The scouts followed outdoor pursuits like signalling, trails and cooking, and often included hikes down to Malpas and back to college by going across the river on the ferry to St Michael Penkivel. It was not long before the numbers grew and the Peewit patrol was added to those of the Wood Pigeons, Stags and Owls. The first camp was held at Whitsun in 1928, on Hayle Towans.

In March 1928 the Wolf Cub pack was set up for younger members of the school, led by Mrs Jervis, the first form mistress. 'The newly-invested cubs gave vent to their feelings of joy in the Grand Howl' and other students were warned that '…with ears upright, sharp wide-awake eyes, and a wolfish grin, these nineteen Cubs are roaming the College, and seeking adventure and opportunities for service'[17]. The cubs were presented with a wolf head totem pole as a competition prize to promote keenness in the pack. Not long afterwards a Rover Crew was formed for the more senior boys.

During the summer of 1928 the Heard Bowl Competition, a county competition for scouts, was held, in which the participants had to undertake sig-nalling, tracking and hiking. The final was held at the estate of Lieutenant Colonel Trefusis and was between the 4th Falmouth Troop, the Penzance St John's Troop and the troop from Truro College. The long distance signalling and two miles at Scout pace test was won by Truro College and Penzance won the tracking test. Overall, however, Truro won on total number of points, and Penzance were run-ners up. At a scout athletics meet in June 1929, John Fitzherbert became the first College scout to be awarded the King's Scout honour. By this time the scouting movement had become as popular in the school as the Cadet Corps had been ten years previously.

The school was still expanding and in 1925 Sir Josiah Stamp, attended by Magson in his new doctorate robes, opened more new buildings. The former carpentry workshop had been turned into a physics laboratory, while the workshop had been transferred to the lower playground. There were also new music rooms and four new classrooms – two in the former library and two on the lower floor of the new building. The reference library was relo-cated to a dormitory on the first floor, with a small room at one end for a fiction library.

The most notable building work was the new

The ceremony for laying the foundation stone of the chapel in 1927, attended by Edward, Prince of Wales (courtesy of *The Times*)

The Prince of Wales overseeing the placement of the foundation stone

school hall and chapel, which was built in 1927-8. Edward, Prince of Wales laid its foundation stone with much ceremony, on 8 June 1927. The students were 'agog with excitement' and it was felt that 'this indeed was the greatest day of our history, for it was the first time a Royal visit had been paid to the School'[18]. The Prince arrived soon after 12 noon and was met by a welcoming party led by the chairman of the governors, Lt.-Col. Stanley Smith and the headmaster. The Prince, with Lt.-Col. T.M. Lowry, inspected a guard of honour made up of more than 70 old boys who had served in the war, before walking to the building site. A dais was erected over the foundation stone, with microphones for speeches and the boys sat within the low foundation walls while guests sat in stands around the edge.

After the divine service Magson addressed the gathering, praising the work of the past headmasters

We look forward to the completion of our new buildings, because we believe that they will enable us, upon the sound foundation laid by these men, to raise a superstructure worthy of this city, and of the Church to which this School belongs … and the new School Hall, which will be our School Chapel, will be a permanent and continued reminder of the supreme aim which the School has set before it, of training boys of sound character and true religion[19].

The Prince then briefly spoke, including that 'he understood that at first the College was intended only for boys from the West of England, but now

Inspection of the guard of honour, made up of old boys who fought in the First World War. The Prince of Wales is accompanied by Lt.-Col. T.M. Lowry

its benefits were open to boys of all parts. In conclusion, he said that he had asked the Headmaster that an extra week might be added to the summer holidays'[20]. He was then presented with a trowel and mallet by the architect, G.E. Withers, and the builder, John Williams, to lay the stone, which was soon declared 'well and truly laid'. On the suggestion of the Prince the mallet and trowel would be kept in the school chapel and he then left to visit the Royal Cornwall Show, at Treliske.

The Chapel was finally opened on 7 December 1928 by Lady Smith, widow of Sir George Smith, led by a guard of honour from the College Scouts[21]. The chapel window incorporated the coat of arms of the Prince of Wales, to commemorate the laying of the foundation stone. The old school room, pre-

viously the main assembly room, was converted into three classrooms with a dormitory above and in addition to the new buildings, the playing fields increased in size, with waste bits of ground landscaped into gardens. It seemed quite remarkable that less than fifty years previously 'the site was then nothing but an uncultivated field…'[22]. reflecting the rapid expansion of the school, and of Truro itself.

The Masters' Feast was introduced in 1921 by Bert Willday, as a 'winding-up supper' for the end of the autumn term. At the end would be an entertainment, often a play, put on by the masters. This eventually led to the school's first public performance of a school play. Magson's birthday was also celebrated with a feast and in 1927 it coincided with Empire Day. The subsequent repast was

The stone laying service.

enthusiastically met by the students, who, as always were led by their stomachs. 'To say the tables groaned under the good things would be an exaggeration; tables only did such things as that in Elizabethan times, but they held as much as any self-respecting table should'[23].

The Old Boys Association had resumed after the war, with a reunion organised by Vinter in 1919. The last meeting before the war had been held in March 1914, but it was not until October 1922 that the next was held, after which the annual cricket match and dinner also recommenced. On 13 November 1923 at Carr's Restaurant in the Strand, the first meeting of the London Branch of the

Truro College Old Boys' Association was held. Its aim, like the original branch, was to maintain links with the College, principally for old boys resident in London. A.L. Potts was elected as chairman of the new branch, with B.F.W. Snow as vice-chairman. Their first annual dinner was held on 28 February 1924 at Gattis Restaurant in the Strand and was followed by musical entertainment. The second annual meeting was followed by 'a smoking concert' in which the school song was sung 'very enthusiastically' and a small sketch entitled 'Box and Cox' performed by Yelland, W.A. Boggia and H.T. Pearson was included amidst the subsequent musical recitals[24].

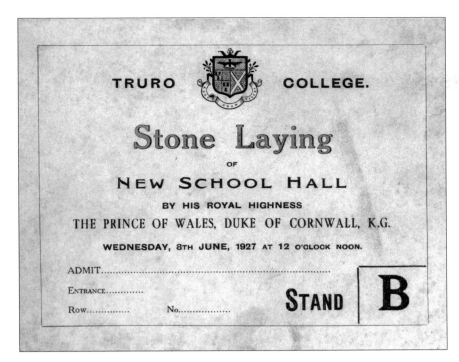

TRURO COLLEGE.

Stone Laying

OF

NEW SCHOOL HALL

BY HIS ROYAL HIGHNESS

THE PRINCE OF WALES, DUKE OF CORNWALL, K.G.

WEDNESDAY, 8TH JUNE, 1927 AT 12 O'CLOCK NOON.

ADMIT..

ENTRANCE..............

Row.............. No................

STAND **B**

Invitations were sent out to local dignitaries, old boys and parents

School life was not always looked back on through rose-tinted spectacles. When D.R. Bray was at the College from 1919 to 1923 he found that he did not escape

the penalties for being new that await boys the world over...crowning the new boys. After supper there was singing. You were driven up on to a desk by the denizens of the Third and forced to pipe up a solo, goaded to your loudest, thin despairing effort by raps on the back of your bare knees with a ruler, enduring meantime a fusillade of chalk and catapult pellets. There was roasting before the big schoolroom stove, and dark hintings of Jimsky, the ghost who haunted the tower...'Squib' Trevethan ran away twice that first term at Truro ... we six faced a hostile world shoulder to shoulder and began to enjoy school, despite a Spartan existence.... It was behind the 'sanny' that we juniors fought out our differences ...bleeding noses, tears almost but not quite suppressed, then firm friendship. The older boys settled their quarrels in the gym, with boxing gloves and a referee ...25.

The school magazine received an overhaul in 1922 when boys were permitted to act as editors for the first time. The first student editors were L.F. Fairchild and C.D. Webb. The magazine had been previously run and mostly written by the teachers, but this changed after a meeting with sixth formers to discuss its literary scope and ability26. The meeting led to the inclusion of more light-hearted articles - 'Our domestic staff seems at times too bright for our sober ways – and their propensity for ragtime sometimes offends the musical ear of the Editor, even when heard through two thick walls. Still, as he genially reminds us, even we were young once'27. There were even some practical jokes. In 1926 it featured a short-lived archaeological club, headed by Tom Magson, the headmaster's son, which was established after the apparent discovery of a sheep-skin scroll near the College. It was reported that an expert from the British Museum found that 'the parchment is so ancient that the script is almost illegible', but he managed to decipher a few passages. It was reported to contain 'The Book of the Prophecy of Iamanass the prophet, son of Iamano his father'. It depicted the expansion of a 'palace' '...upon the Hill' because the number of people within had increased too much, so the 'Ruler' 'caused to be brought to him his Staff of Office and he called together the wise men so that they might take counsel together what they might do...' It was not long before 'then began a great Dumping of Stuff for the building, until the court-yard of the Palace was like unto a Muck-Heap and

Above – 1928 school cricket team.
Back row: R.S. Nicholls, A.T. Williams, F.L. Stephens, D.E. Munro, A.T.D. Green, L.F. Brewer, J.C.B. Daniel.
Front row: E. Revill (fast bowler), W.R.C. Smith (fast bowler), A.F. Pownall (captain, slow bowler), E.M. Brown (stump and big scorer 80-100), G.N. Smith.
Right – 1922 school football team. Back row: F.J. Barnes, C.T. Nicholls, V.T. Higgins, S. Orchard, F.W.M. Hearle, J.G. Barrett, G. White, A.B. Hamson. Front row: L.F. Fairchild, R.C. Webb, P. Pearce, A.J. Dixon, G.F. Coon.

the people of the ruler wist not where to put their feet withal'[28]. It does not take a great leap of imagination to guess that this was comment on the continual expansion of the school and what must have seemed like perpetual building work.

In July 1924 the magazine celebrated its 100th edition, at which time approximately 450 copies were produced each term, costing half a crown for an annual subscription, and since 1921 copies had been held at the British Museum. The next major change was to its name in 1926 when the *Truro College Magazine* became *The Truronian*.

The clubs and societies within the school became much more varied as new groups were formed. On the encouragement of the headmaster, a garden club was set up in April 1922 and the participants were allowed the use of an area of school ground for vegetables and flowers[29]. A geography society was started in the spring of 1926 in response to the needs of the sixth form advanced geography class and included various trips both local and abroad. The fur and feather society claimed 30 to 40 members, consisting mainly of pigeon fanciers[30].

Views of the school during the 1920s, before and after the chapel was built.

A lecture on Toc H was given a warm response in January 1928. Its name came from the army signallers' abbreviation for Talbot House. It was established by a padre, Reverend Phillip 'Tubby' Clayton during the war at Poperinghe, near Ypres, 'in memory of one Gilbert Talbot, who seemed to sum up in his character all the best qualities of the British race. Talbot House was entirely at the service of the troops. It was not established for profit, or 'to get, but to give'[31]. and to bring 'a corner of heaven into the hell of men's lives'[32]. It was revived after the war to maintain links between the

School drama productions from the annual concert in 1925, a forerunner of the annual school play.
Below - A scene from *X=O: A tale of the Trojan War.* **Above** - A scene from *The History of Henry IV*

TRURO COLLEGE.

ANNUAL CONCERT.

Friday, March 13th, 1925.

Saturday, March 14th, 1925.

The Committee tenders its heartiest thanks to the Matron and Mrs. Lobb and the other ladies who have assisted in the making of the costumes.

"X = O." *A tale of the Trojan War.*

by John Drinkwater.

CAST:

Pronax	Greeks	J. R. Barnard.
Salvius	Greeks	R. H. Tregunna.
Ilus	Trojans	R. J. M. Wilkes
Capys	Trojans	R. Orchard.
Sentinel		R. Osborne.
Slave		V. T. L. Roberts.

Scene I. The Greek Camp before Troy.
Scene II. On Troy Wall.
Scene III. The Greek Tent again.
Scene IV. The Trojan Wall.

Scenes from

"*The History of Henry the Fourth,*"

by William Shakespeare.

(Being the humorous Conceits of Sir John Falstaff.)

DRAMATIS PERSONÆ:

Henry, Prince of Wales	R. Hambly.
Poins (his friend)	R. S. Nicholls.
Sir John Falstaff	Mr. G. Stanley.
Gadshill	G. N. Minifie.
Bardolph	T. S. Magson.
Peto	A. B. Barnard.
Travellers	J. R. Luke. R. B. S. Rose.
Francis (a drawer)	J. F. C. Probert.
Vintner	J. L. Normansell.
Mistress Quickly (hostess of the Boar's Head)	A. S. Wilkes.
Sheriff	F. E. Emmett.
Carrier	R. H. Rosewarne.

The Actors are named in order of appearance.

The Two Plays will be performed on each occasion, and Selections from the following Programme of Music will be made:

Choir.—2 Part Songs— "Tinkers' Song" ... *Howells.*
"True Story" ... *Howells.*
Unison— "My Boy Billy"
"Dashing away with the smoothing iron"
"Chequered Career"
"Lasses of Scotland"

Pianoforte Duets.—"Casse Noisette Suite" *Tchaikowsky.*
"March" ... *Mendlessohn.*
Mr. Way and C. R. Evans.

Solo.— "Claire de lune" (*Debussy*) Mr. Way, A.R.C.O.

Recitations.—Form I.

Jordan, Truro.

Above - The schoolroom set up as a theatre
Bottom - Programme for the entertainment

survivors and to let the next generation share in it. The society existed for comradeship, service, fair-mindedness and the spread of the Gospel by living it and not preaching it. As a result the Regnal League was set up in 1929, a junior branch of Toc H; with the 'Circle of Pals' for boys aged 13 to 15[33]. It was the first of its kind to be established in a public school.

By 1923 there was increasing interest in the new form of radio. An aerial was fixed to the flagpole and connected to apparatus in the sixth form study. There seemed to be little initial success because 'the two would-be 'listeners-in' both insist on fiddling with the tuning adjustments at the same time, the result being ear-piercing shrieks, birds twittering presumably on the aerial, dogs barking furiously, and a myriad of indescribable sounds as are beyond all human ken'[34]. Over-enthusiasm led to essential pieces breaking off and the battery wearing out, leading to the radio set being returned home for its own safety. During April 1924, a wireless club was formed by enthusiasts, who were loaned a crystal set by Mr Ault, and a 'clothes line' was stretched across the top playground. The main interest was in the reception of Morse code. However it was not long before the radio was used to enhance revision for boys studying for matriculation, who 'enjoyed a series of lectures broadcast from London by Mr A.W.P. Gayford, on Modern European History'[35]. A camera club was re-established during the early 1920s, and arranged photography competitions, but

Egbert Hockey Magson, the fourth headmaster.

E.H. Magson (1921 - 1946)

Egbert Hockey Magson, the son of a Wesleyan schoolmaster[1], was a student of King Edward's School, Birmingham and gained the Heslop Memorial Scholarship at Birmingham University. After gaining his B.Sc. in 1901 he studied for the Teachers' Diploma of the London University at Westminster Training College, under Dr Workman. After his training he became a science master, specialising in chemistry and physics. He was then appointed master of method and a lecturer at Westminster Training College, where his record was 'one of strenuous endeavour in the case of education'. He continued his academic research work with various papers on 'dynamic isomerism' and which were published by the Chemical Society. In 1915 Magson gained a place on the 1st class honours list and the following year gained an M.A. from London University. Despite a keen interest in soccer and hockey, his health proved to be his 'one anxiety' and prevented him from taking up military service in the First World War. However he undertook many varied wartime activities; he became vice president of the Westminster Training College for teachers, ran the Petersham Russell School, as well as teaching science at Tiffins School, acted as secretary to the Richmond Education Committee, and still found some spare time to cultivate an allotment[2].

Magson came to Truro College in 1921; his wife Emily was Cornish by birth, having been raised in Tregony. Both his sons attended the school becoming head prefects and participating in the school football and cricket teams. In 1925 Magson was awarded a doctorate in Science of Psychology by the University of London after 12 years research work in experimental psychology and theoretical chemistry. To celebrate the occasion the school presented him with doctorate robes of scarlet and gold. Soon after Dr Magson was appointed the Senate of London University's representative to the board of governors of the University College of the South West at Exeter.

During Dr Magson's term of office at Truro the school was greatly extended, with several new buildings including the chapel, a science block, and boarding houses for junior pupils, the playing fields were levelled and Treliske was acquired as a preparatory school. Dr Magson was also a prominent freemason, who was a founder and the fifth Master of the Epworth Lodge, London, and a founder of the Truro School Lodge and was its first Worshipful Master in 1936. In 1940 he was appointed to the rank of Past Assistant Grand Director of Ceremonies in the United Grand Lodge of England, and was Provincial Grand Chaplain of the Province of Kent[3].

During the Second World War Magson invited Kent College to stay at the school, and he continued to lead the school through the hardships of war, despite being well overdue for retirement. Consequently he retired from the post of headmaster in 1946. He spent his last years in Dover with his wife, moving from Truro in 1950. He died on 6 August 1961 and a memorial plaque was unveiled at Truro School, on the external wall of the school chapel, in the 1990s[4].

Mrs Magson's Bible Class

…Mrs Magson, ran a class on Sunday afternoons. Attendance was voluntary, but attendance excused us from prep … Mrs Magson was a fervent supporter of the British Women's Total Abstinence Union and of the temperance cause. Every Sunday afternoon she would get a boy to bring the banner of the Truro branch of the B.W.T.A.U. [later the 'White Ribbon Association'] into the School Chapel where it was proudly displayed for all to see.

It was mainly the younger boys who stayed for the class. She was a kindly lady and not very good at keeping discipline among 50 or 60 unruly young-sters…Her main theme, to which much time was devoted, was the temperance cause. However she was never strident, and … a kindly and matronly lady.

From an article by F. Chappel printed in the Truro School Former Pupils' Association Newsletter, February 2001.

Domestic Staff in July 1938

Daily:	Wages	Age
Head Cook: Mrs Penrose	27s 6d weekly	
Head Scullery and Pantry Maid: Millie Purdie	21/- weekly	
Laundry: Phyllis Lawry	15/- weekly	29
Pantry and Dining Hall: Winifred Harris	12s 6d weekly	
General Help: Dorothy Barnicoat	16/- weekly	36
Workroom Help (Occasional): Mrs Richards		

Resident:		
Headmaster's House: Annie Lobb	£33 per annum	
Staff Maid: Hyacinth Lawrence	£36 per annum	20
First Housemaid: Ann Terrell	£28 16s per annum	18
Second Housemaid: May Berryman	£24 per annum	17
Epworth Housemaid: Joyce Matthews	£22 16s per annum	18
Pentreve Housemaid: Doreen Batten	£16 16s per annum	15
Second Scullery Maid: Kathleen Moses	£18 per annum	
Dormitory Maid: Louise Eva	£36 per annum	
Between Maid: Doris Allen	£16 per annum	15
Kitchen Maid: Peggy Trethewey	£20 8s per annum	14

Male staff (all daily):		
Engines, boilers and outside work: Mr W. Penrose		
Assistant to Mr Penrose: Leslie Keast, formerly houseboy	11s 6d weekly	15
Gardens: Mr Stephens		
Mr Trembarth, formerly houseboy	10/- weekly	
Pentreve: Harding		
Science Block: Trethewey		

1930-1939

Truro School in 1934 (courtesy of Aerofilms)

1930 - 1939: Truro School

T he early 1930s saw a change to the school's name and status. In 1931, although having just celebrated its golden jubilee, and although the name of Truro College was widely known, public opinion had altered so that it was 'now considered somewhat pretentious for any Educational Institution to claim the style of "College" if its pupils are for the most part below the age of 18'. Consequently, following a resolution passed by the Methodist

A new version of the school crest to mark the change of the school's name from Truro College to Truro School

Education Committee, which recommended that all its boarding schools should adopt the form of 'school' rather than 'college', Truro College became Truro School. This would also help relieve the confusion of the postal service and visitors that had existed, because the Diocesan Training College was officially known as Truro College by the Board of Education. The school magazine also reflected this change, renaming itself *The Truronian: The Magazine of Truro School*[1].

In 1934, the school was given the distinction of becoming a public school by the Head Masters' Conference. The number of public schools was limited by the association to 150 and 'admission to and continuance of membership depends upon the scheme under which the school is administered, taking into account particularly the measure of independence enjoyed by the governing body and the headmaster...' and the number of pupils staying on for higher education and going on to university[2].

Throughout the mid 1930s the arguments over the lack of choice for secondary education for boys from Truro re-emerged. There was concern that Truro had not been provided with a council-run secondary school when the system was set up in 1906. At the time the city had been sufficiently catered for by Truro College, which although not under the county authority's jurisdiction had similar fees to county schools[3]. However the fees had risen

by the 1930s and the rise to public school status, which enhanced its appeal, meant that it could no longer be expected for the school to take all boys from Truro and the surrounding district, because of the demand put on places[4]. The *West Briton* commented:

For many years the county education authority has saved an enormous amount of money through the slight contribution which they made to Truro School, amounting to £720 per year. That meant that the county had had education for 120 day boys at Truro School at a cost of about £6 per head, whereas the cost of secondary education for boys and girls throughout the county was £17 16s 9d per head[5].

TRURO COLLEGE
OLD BOYS' ASSOCIATION

JUBILEE CELEBRATION

ANNUAL DINNER

Friday, January 10th, 1930.

Chairman :— E. P. ADAMS, Esq.

A. B. PARRETT, } Joint
E. S. VINCENT, } Hon. Secs.

The jubilee of the school was widely celebrated by past and present pupils. This dinner programme also shows the old style crest

The problem still remained unsolved; it was reported that half the difference between Truro School and County School fees would be paid by the local education district to those parents affected[6].

Rugby football was reintroduced during the 1931 Easter term, initially as an experiment to gauge the enthusiasm for it. It was not intended to replace soccer, as soccer had done to rugby in 1890, but to give boys a wider choice and opportunity of finding a suitable sport for themselves. The new side showed a lot of promise but speed and direction needed the most practise. It was not long before the school magazine was singing the praises of the new game 'by playing this game boys are taught to be kind to animals and grow into peace-loving Englishmen, because they discover what an awful thing is war. Besides, bull-fighting is illegal in England'[7]. New playing fields were acquired to create adequate rugby pitches. The first school team included teachers among the players because the lack of school clubs meant that the team had to play established town clubs. By 1934 it was still necessary to travel to Devon to play most of the school matches[8], because of a lack of school rugby teams in Cornwall.

New school colours were adopted in the summer of 1930, primarily worn by prefects and members of the cricket team, though the whole school was to wear the new blazer and cap with matching scarves and ties in September. The bottle green blazers with the crest on the breast pocket were replaced by blazers of '....a dark royal blue base, with chocolate stripes three-tenths of an inch wide, lined with white, and two and three-tenths of an inch apart'[9]. Eton collars, Marlborough suits and mortarboards were still worn on Sundays for morning services. The custom of school leavers throwing their mortarboards into the river from

Right - The school rugby team, the first since 1882. Back row: W. Fitzherbert, H.J. Martin, J.H.H. Magson, J.C. Nicholls, D.G. Brown, D. McKinney, A. Stephens, P.R. Stevens, F.N. Blamey. Middle row: R.C. Barrett, D.R. Robinson, D.B. McKinney (captain), T.M. de Lange, R.W. Sawyer. Front row: R.D. Morton, I.B. Rae

Above - Epworth boarding house, named after the birthplace of John Wesley

Bottom - Pentreve boarding house, opened in 1930

The opening of Epworth House May 1934

Boscawen Bridge on their final Sunday was well established by the end of the 1930s[10].

Collections were annually made for several charities including the Royal Life Boat Institution, the National Children's Home and Orphanage, and Armistice Day. In addition, an annual scholarship was raised of twenty pounds by pupils and sent through a Mission House to the Wesley College, in Wuchang, China, for a school leaver entering the Central China University. Its objective was to provide teaching staff for the college with a university education. The Chinese government offered five scholarships for the whole of the country for a course at an English University for four years. In 1930 two out of the five were awarded to students at the Central China University, helped by the Truro College scholarship. The first recipient was Li Ch'un Kwang[11].

Since 1921 the school had grown to cover 23 and a half acres with an additional 14 acres of playing fields rented. The new buildings included the chapel, play room, three dormitories, the junior house and the second master's house. The old buildings had been divided into more classrooms, improving on the four classes in 1921. Hot water appliances had been installed through all the classrooms and dormitories, except the science block, and two gas engines were used to generate electric light. In 1935 the school was floodlit by electric light for the first time. During the 1930s the school expanded still further. A new racquet court, named the Turner court, was dug out and the levelling of the playing fields continued. On 17 July 1939 a bathing pavilion was opened at Loe Beach to facilitate changing for swimming practise and the annual swimming gala.

The main additions to the school at this time were the boarding houses, needed to accommodate the increased number of pupils in the school. Pentreve, adjoining the Junior House, was purchased in 1930 to cater for boys under eleven, the garage in the grounds was converted for the cubs' headquarters and it was not long before plans were made for a new boarding house for boys of the middle school. Epworth was opened in May 1934 to accommodate 24 boys[12].

Treliske, which opened as a self-contained junior boarding house in 1936

Despite the new additions to the boarding accommodation it was not long until it was necessary to make additional arrangements. Pentreve was taken over for the expanding middle school, so consequently Treliske, the former home of Sir George Smith, was purchased and modified for the junior boys. Briefly before this the Junior House was opened in The Parade[13]. Margaret Smith, daughter of Sir George and sister to Lt.-Col. Stanley Smith became a school governor at this time and the school magazine noted that 'the advantage of having a Lady Governor has already been made manifest in the task of furnishing and equipping Treliske'[14]. Electric light, a new hot water system and central heating was installed as well as the laying out of rooms for dormitories and classrooms.

Treliske was opened as a junior house of Truro School in May 1936, with 33 pupils. Thomas 'Tommy' Stratton acted as housemaster and taught Form 2, his wife Helena taught Form 1 and Miss Parry took the position of matron. The school fees were £13 10s a term for boarders and £8 a term for day pupils. The boys were divided into two houses within Treliske – Sparta and Athens – and the competition was most noticeable between them in the summer sports day, first won by Sparta. Although the boys lived entirely at Treliske and had there lessons there, the connection with the Main School was maintained, with certain teachers visiting Treliske for lessons and the boys taken to the school for all functions and important sports matches[15].

Aside from the work aspect of life at Treliske the boys got up to many activities and games, often quite mischievous. John Bridger recalled that 'camp and hut building and gang warfare in the wood were our main amusements. I recall David Webb being hit in the mouth by a bamboo spear but there were no fatalities!' Stories of the early years at Treliske also included the collecting of 'lost' golf balls, from the neighbouring golf course, some of which were not actually lost and eating dog biscuits belonging to Tommy Stratton's dog, Punch, especially the black ones. One pastime involved a model field gun, which fired caps and with which boys '…devised a

Above - Prize giving at Treliske sports' day, 1936
Below - Treliske football team, 1938

Top - A scene from *Charley's Aunt*, with Cyril 'Freddie' Wilkes on the sofa
Bottom - The curtain call for *Charley's Aunt* performed in 1938

method of loading the shell case with red matches and a bagatelle steel ball and were able to fire it against the inside of the library door – I expect the dents are still there'[16]. Boys in the Main School appear to have been less fortunate in their mischief making, with punishments given for walking on piano keys, carrying letters from a maid at Pentreve to one of the boys, robbing an orchard and carving a name on the chapel wall, in addition to the usual tales of disorderly behaviour, bullying, smoking and swearing[17].

The school was inspected in 1934 and it was noted that the curriculum had recently been changed to a half yearly syllabus. As a result the classes were reconstituted each February and September. In February the better boys were moved to the 'A' Forms, so that Form Va took the July exam for the School Certificate and Form V took the same exam in December. It therefore took either four, four and a half or five years to study for the School Certificate depending on ability[18]. An emphasis was laid upon the sciences, mathematics and geography, though a wide range of foreign languages were provided and the school was one of a small number teaching modern European history, which was considered essential if the boys were to take part in the 'government of their country when they grow up'[19]. Bible lessons were still held weekly, but scripture exams had been given up in the early 1920s; endorsing Magson's belief that religion was 'an atmosphere to be breathed and a life to be lived' and that, though it was a Methodist school, sectarian instruction should not be given[20].

The non-academic side of school life continued to develop with new clubs and societies being formed. The chess club was revived in early 1933, and its popularity led the school magazine to quip 'life is at all times a risky business, but just lately a new and terrifying danger has been added to the list. We are beset on every side by Chess Men'[21]. A bee-keeping society was formed in the summer of 1934, to which the headmaster presented 'a vigorous swarm and several hives'. By the end of term 17lbs of honey had been collected[22]. The first full school play, 'Charley's Aunt', was held in the spring of 1938, as a spin off from the previous Masters'

Feast. This consequently led to the formation of the dramatic society and it was not long before the plays became an annual event[23]. An entertainments committee was formed in 1933 to provide amusement for boarders on Saturday evenings. The various programmes included concerts, talks, plays and Charles Miller 'with his projector, has introduced 'Movies' to the school'[24].

During the 1930s there was a growing interest in cars, since they were becoming an increasingly common sight. Mr Brock, a languages teacher, acted as the staff chauffeur. An article on how to be a motorist suggested that '...no motorist worthy of the proud name would be seen gliding around the countryside in a travelling drawing room'. Similarly the writer extolled the benefits of a small car; 'it can be steered under lorries, between pedestrians' legs, and can be garaged in the dog-kennel'. The actual driving of a car was considered 'simple'.

The whole art in driving a car consists in turning the wheel so that the car follows the general direction of the road, and in pulling or pushing a lever or two at the appropriate time so that the car is kept in motion. The horn, bell or klaxon must be kept continually at work[25].

A few years later there was a report of a 'yellow and black shape' speeding up the drive at 100mph and despite 'many set backs, the motoring brotherhood in Truro School has grown into a world-famed organisation with the motto 'Per ardua ad astra'[26]. The enthusiasm for motoring was especially marked within the Old Boys' Association, which produced a car badge with the school crest and started an annual motor run around the Cornish coast.

The College scout and cub packs were renamed the 1st Truro School pack, soon after the school changed its name. In 1933 several scouts attended the fourth world jamboree in Budapest. While travelling by train to Hungary, they stopped briefly in Germany where '...the courtesy of the Nazi Yungten and storm troopers was again shown, when they provided us with excellent coffee from an army kitchen which they brought on the platform'. At the jamboree the scouts studied woodcraft, visited the

Above - Leaving for a trip to Germany in the 1938 Easter holidays
Below - A tour around the Stalactite Caves of Rubeland in Germany

camp theatre or roamed the town, including a visit to the mineral baths. There were also excursions to Debrecin, Lake Balaton, local chocolate factories, breweries and farms on the Danube River. 'The Jamboree… was a great success. The nations really mixed and you might quite often spend a whole afternoon in the company of a Swiss, Austrian or Hungarian scout'[27]. Four years later a delegation from Truro School also went to the fifth jamboree held in Holland.

By the end of the decade, even though tensions were slowly gathering in Europe, school trips abroad continued, often with a sense of promoting good feeling between the countries. Despite Germany annexing Austria in March 1938, 32 boys and three masters travelled to there that Easter, staying in Berlin and Wernigerode in the Harz Mountains. The trip included sightseeing at the palace of Sans Souci, in Potsdam, and to the stalactite caves of Rubeland.

On another occasion the boys were the guests of the Anglo-German Club of Berlin, and were later cordially welcomed by leaders of the Youth Movement at two of their camps. There they were well entertained, playing football, exchanging songs, and learning folk dances from the Hitler Youth…During the whole of their stay in Germany they met with the utmost consideration and kindness. The impression the boys brought back with them was one of friendliness, hospitality and good-will[28].

The following year an Easter trip was organised again to Paris, previously visited in 1937, consisting of sight-seeing and visiting the theatre. Unlike the trip to Germany there was less personal contact with the people of the country. Freddie Wilkes noted that

the chief value of the trip lay … in the apprehension of a totally different civilisation …to broaden understandings and create opportunities for practising the language; …the bolder spirits, once they had overcome their natural shyness, did dare to pronounce a little of their home-grown French, and naturally reaped no small satisfaction, when they were finally understood[29].

An Old Boy's Song
1. *High on the hill uplifted,*
O'er river, bridge and Town
The grey old Tower and Gables
Of Truro School look down;

And there in happy friendship
We lived our youthful days
Come raise your tuneful voices
And sing aloud her praise.

Chorus: Long live the good old School, boys,
Let all good fellows sing,
Long live the name of Truro
And honour to her bring.

2. *In classroom, field and dormy,*
We learned to play the game
And 'esse quam videri'
Our rule of life became;
In triumph ever modest
In failure ne'er cast down
We strove, while self forgetting
To bring our School renown

3. *Thro'out the world we're scattered*
O'er many seas and lands
Yet clear in memory's vision
That grey old building stands;
It nerves to fresh endeavour
Its message still the same
'However stern the conflict,
Fight on, and play the game!'

4. *Some comrades true have left us*
Their work already done
Strong souls, whose tasks were ended
Before the setting sun;
Their memory inspires us
To carry on the fight
For all they loved and cherished
For Honour and the Right.

5. *Old Time is on our track, boys*
The years are fleeting fast
Still much must be accomplished
'Ere we lay down our task;
For Truro's fame and glory
We'll keep the ancient rule
And win fresh laurels for her
God bless the good old school![32]

Several well-known people were connected with the school in this decade. Sir Arthur Quiller-Couch had been on the board of governors for nearly twenty years when he resigned in 1937 due to ill health[30]. In July 1938 T.S. Elliot was the visiting guest of honour at Speech Day and wrote an article in the subsequent school magazine[31].

In 1933, a song, specially written for the old boys of the school, was sung for the first time by the choir at Speech Day. It was an attempt to give the Association an increased sense of unity, although it did not appear to catch on as the old school song did.

By 1939, the Old Boys' Association had lost several of its older members including Tom Wickett, an early pupil, Association chairman in 1926 and a school governor for 35 years. In 1937, an electric clock, given by his widow, was installed in the school tower in his memory[33]. The Truro School Freemasons' Lodge was established in 1936, encouraged by Magson who was installed as the first master.

The peaceful life at the school was not to last for long. The outbreak of war in September 1939 brought further change and upheaval, with rationing, restrictions and evacuees.

The Masters' Feast in 1934, held at the end of term just before Christmas since the early 1920s

Treliske

Treliske was built by William Teague, a mine captain, on land known as the 'Liskes' in the mid nineteenth century[1]. Teague was a self-made man, who had worked his way up through the mining industry from boyhood. The property, bought by George Smith of the firm of Bickford-Smith and Co. in 1886, was a spacious mansion, with five family bedrooms, and six servants' rooms off a separate staircase. The particulars of the sale included a description of the ornamental porch, a fernery and palm house leading off the dining room and a 'lofty conservatory', as well as the usual range of day rooms including morning, billiard, and drawing rooms and a library. The gardens included a vinery, a forcing house and a peach and nectarine house as well as a pond, glasshouses and a variety of fruit trees.

In 1897 Queen Victoria gave George Smith a knighthood in recognition for his business success as a vase manufacturer and merchant, his service as a Justice of the Peace and recognition for the promotion of Methodism in Cornwall. Born in Camborne, and related to the Bickford-Smiths of Trevarno, he married Jane Symons Burgess, and lived at Treliske with his children and parents-in-law[2]. Several members of his family served as governors to the school. Sir George was the first in 1904, though he had been connected to the school since its foundation in 1879. Colonel G.E. Stanley Smith succeeded his father as chairman of the governors in 1921. His sister Margaret joined the board of governors in the 1930s, initially to help with the refurbishment of Treliske after its purchase by the school in 1934. A cousin, Graham Burrell Smith, succeeded Colonel Smith as chairman of the governors in 1948. He held the position for over 15 years, and was the seventh member of his extended family to serve on the board of governors.

By the early 1930s it became apparent that more boarding accommodation was needed; boys were using part of the sickroom for beds. After much discussion over options, it was decided that Treliske House would be suitable for the purpose; Dr Magson and Dr Workman inspected the site in November 1935, and thought it 'eminently suitable for a Preparatory School for little boys', able to accommodate 26 boarders.

The projected costs for reconditioning Treliske in 1935:

1. For bringing in the Gas and Water mains	£175
2. For bringing in the Electric cable	£165
3. For wiring Treliske for electricity	£50
4. For the provision of Gas Fires	£33
5. For the provision of Gas Cookers (in enamel finish)	£56
6. For the provision of a Hot Water Supply by Gas	£150
7. For providing the necessary WC's, pipes etc	£100
8. For painting and decorating Treliske	£200
Total	**£929**

Treliske Fees for 1936

21 guineas per term for the 15 boys present in Truro School who would be transferred to Treliske.

25 guineas per term for boarders going to Truro School after Treliske

29 guineas per term for boarder going elsewhere after Treliske

6 guineas per term for day boys going to Truro School after Treliske

10 guineas per term for day boys going elsewhere after Treliske.

1940-1949

1940 - 1949:
Truro School during World War Two

By June 1939, Magson reported that although 'the School is very fortunately situated in what is probably one of the safest places in the whole of the country'; precautionary measures had been carried out, including the fitting of gas masks, frequent fire drills and the sunken lane and concrete reinforced basement of the science block were to be used as 'blast-proof shelters'. The relative safety of Truro's position meant that from early on there was an increased number of applications for boarders from the London area[1]. The headmaster also talked of 'active pacifism' and its role as 'preventative medicine for the body politic', with war as the last resort[2].

After war was declared in September, a constant effort was made to maintain the numerous out of school activities and any difficulties were slightly alleviated by an increased number of town and weekend permits granted. New activities included sentry duty around the school from dusk to bedtime.

A School that is set on a hill cannot be hid. We have hundreds of windows, a single gleam can be seen for miles, and curtains are easily disarranged when healthy are about. Half an hour's marching up and down a beat on a dark winter night is neither thrilling nor pleasant, even when a sentry-box is provided, but the duty is done with few grumbles[3].

A Typical Menu during Rationing

Monday.
Breakfast – Boiled Eggs, Bread and Butter.
Dinner – Corned Beef, Baked Potatoes,
Steamed Fruit Pudding and Custard.
Tea – Cheese and Potato Cake,
Bread and Butter.

Tuesday.
Breakfast – Porridge, Jam, Bread and Butter.
Dinner – Roast Lamb, Greens, Potatoes,
Semolina Pudding
Tea – Cornflakes with milk, Bread and Butter.

Wednesday.
Breakfast – Bacon, Fried Bread,
Bread and Butter.
Dinner – Sausages, Beans, Potatoes, plain
Steamed Pudding and Treacle.
Tea – Spaghetti Pie, Bread and Butter.

Thursday.
Breakfast – Shredded Wheat – Potted Meat,
Bread and Butter.
Dinner – Roast Beef, Greens, Potatoes,
Mince Pies
Tea – Cheese, Bread and Butter

Friday.
Breakfast – Cornflakes, Sausage Rolls,
Bread and Butter.
Dinner – Soup, Mixed Vegetables,
Baked Potatoes, Jam Tarts.
Tea – Baked Potatoes with Margarine,
Bread and Butter.

Saturday.
Breakfast – Porridge, Marmalade,
Bread and Butter.
Dinner – Cottage Pie, Greens,
Baked Bread-and-Butter Pudding
Tea – Chicken and Ham Roll, Bread and
Butter.

Sunday.
Breakfast – Cornflakes, Jam, Bread and Butter.
Dinner – Cold Lamb, Baked Potatoes,
Prunes and Custard.
Tea – Buns or Cake, Bread and Butter.
Supper every night – Milk and Biscuits.

Compared with the 1914 -1918 war the school magazine quickly felt the affects this time; reports were curtailed and fewer pages were printed as publishers raised the cost of production[4]. Sports matches continued and included some against evacuated schools, such as Marylebone Grammar School and Sutton Secondary School. Unlike the previous war, universal national service largely protected the sixth form from the pressure to enlist that had been faced by their predecessors in 1914. They were now encouraged to finish their education and even to start university before joining the Forces. 'The attitude of the authorities this time has been very definitely to discourage anything in the nature of a recruiting campaign in the Schools'. Instead, senior boys took part in the collection of waste material and various forms of agricultural work. Four acres of the playing fields were ploughed up for extra potatoes and another field was loaned to the Army for the football season[5].

By 1942 the calling up of women for National Service caused some difficulties for the domestic side of the school. The boarders were called upon to help with some of the work like sweeping the dormitories and corridors, while the day boys kept the science block clean. 'It has been freely stated that the rooms were never better kept than at present, but we must remember the old proverb about 'New brooms', and keep up to this high standard even when the novelty has warn off'.

Rationing made the school menu more restricted but in 1942 it was commented that 'after 2 years of War the U-boat campaign has not been successful in causing us to go hungry ... When butter is referred to, it means, of course, a mixture of butter and margarine, and we should naturally be glad if the meat ration were bigger'[6].

The most considerable change to school life was the arrival of Kent College, an associate Methodist school evacuated from Canterbury, in the summer term of 1940. Initially they were given a number of classrooms to hold their own lessons, but by 1941, due to the increased number of teachers enlisting, Kent College was absorbed and integrated into the school and was known as Kent College House, retaining its uniform of blue and maroon blazers[7]. The father of P.W. Richards, second master of Kent College, had been one of the original boarders at Truro College[8]. and over the years several other teachers at Truro also taught at Kent College. Earlier links included two headmasters who had taught at Truro College, F.M. Facer, who left in 1883 and A. Brownscombe who succeeded him in 1911. Several other schools applied for accommodation after Kent College was invited by Magson, but these were turned down due to lack of space. However, Stoke Damerel High School for Girls was able to use the art room, science laboratory, pavilion and playing fields.

The boys enthusiastically took part in the work to help the war effort, including voluntary defence work by some of the day boys and the boarders helping on farmland in the holidays. Harvest Camps were attended by more senior boys, who spent a fortnight west of Penzance helping with the potato harvest. By the summer of 1944 it was planned that 'nearly all boys over 13 will be doing their part in the harvest field'[9]. The Ministry of Agriculture set up a scheme to teach tractor driving to schoolboys, which was undertaken by 40 boys

Saturday entertainment programme from 1941, for both Truro School and Kent College

from Truro School, who were also taught to service a tractor and keep it in order. Other activities included sending books via the Red Cross to prisoners of war, mostly textbooks for matriculation and degree studies, particularly English and Latin classics[10].

Other changes to daily school life included alterations to the school regulations, such as having only one bath a week and the art room roof being used as an observation post by air observation wardens. Several boys had to leave school early to help with family businesses because family members had enlisted and there were staff shortages in all areas of work. There was also a distinct number of war refugees in Truro, including a teacher at Treliske from Prague. There were pupils at Truro School from Germany, Czechoslovakia and Russia. Amongst them was Eric Bauer, a German Jew, who had to leave Truro under the Restrictions for Aliens and moved to Queen's College, Taunton, provided

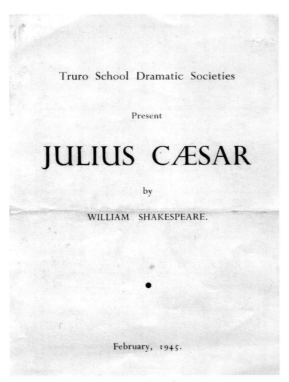

Truro School Dramatic Societies

Present

JULIUS CÆSAR

by

WILLIAM SHAKESPEARE.

•

February, 1945.

for by the Truro School governors. The school remained open to pupils during the holidays, primarily those from Kent College, but also Truro boarders who lived in areas heavily affected by air raids[11].

Many of the clubs and societies continued, including the drama and chess societies, though table tennis had ceased due to a shortage of balls and was replaced with film evenings[12]. The drama society appeared to be one of the highlights of school life, with the annual school play continuing throughout the war years. In addition the Saturday entertainments continued with full programmes combining the talents of Truro School with Kent College. The scout troop lapsed during the war years, but was revived as the 3rd Truro Troop by December 1945[13].

The 1945 school play, *Julius Caesar*, with Robert Shaw as Mark Anthony (standing in the centre). Shaw went on to become a well known film actor

The cast of *Laburnum Grove* by J.B. Priestley, with Truro School and Kent College pupils, c.1941. Left to right: Murch, W. Evans, Beard, René, Beasant, Kendall-Carpenter, J. Bates, Lewis, Norris

An Air Training Corps, Flight 1532, was established at the school, under the command of H. J. Prickett, the headmaster of Kent College. The A.T.C. took the place that the cadet corps had filled in the First World War; it was felt there was not enough staff to act as officers for a cadet corps so 38 boys from Truro School and Kent College joined the Cathedral School corps for drills.

The A.T.C. was attached to a local Naval Air Station, which the cadets visited on several occasions and received instruction on the link trainer, in firing machine guns on the range and in folding and using parachutes, as well as having at least one flight in a glider. They also received lectures from officers every Thursday at school on different aspects of their work, and participated in drills, wireless, morse and navigation classes[14], working towards proficiency exams. Lieutenant Tindall of the Home Guard provided instruction in signalling and the cadets were able to make use of their new skills by acting as signallers in Home Guard exercises[15].

In addition to the skills undertaken in the A.T.C., such as gliding, inter-unit rugby and soccer matches were arranged. In 1944 the School Flight beat the Redruth Unit, but had to retire from the competition due to difficulties incorporating the matches with school fixtures[16]. Members of the A.T.C. took part in an annual summer camp, where they had drills, talks and practises, carried out to a strict daily timetable. The Flight also took part in athletics and after several competitions in 1945 gained three national champions, with T. K. Vivian winning the shot put and the discus, and Ian Goodhand the long jump[17]. J. R. Barker, a sergeant in the A.T.C, was selected to play for England A.T.C. team in a rugby international game against Wales A.T.C. at Cardiff. 'England were beaten, but to Barker fell the honour of scoring the only English try'[18].

The Air Training Corps led by the headmaster of Kent College, H.J. Prickett, who sits, in uniform, between Truro headmaster E.H. Magson and the chairman of the governors Lt.-Col. G.E. Stanley Smith

Truro School boys in the Cathedral School Cadet Corps took part in several field days, which included a mock battle fought in the area around Kea in very hot summer weather, or struggling through deep mud in late autumn. The Corps took part in an annual inspection; in 1942 the Colonel-Commander inspected the Cornwall Cadet Battalion at Trewinard Court, he 'thought that No.5 [which included Truro School] would produce some very efficient Officers'[19].

In addition to the fixtures against Cornish teams there were additional games against evacuated schools. However some sports were more dramatically curtailed. The cricket field on St Clement's Hill was given over to food production, though the school was allowed to fence off the cricket square to protect it. The War Memorial Pavilion was requisitioned for special work in connection with air defence and certain alterations were made such as the installation of gas, water and electricity.

Similarly the Home Guard used the bathing pavilion at Loe Beach throughout the winter as a sleeping place and guardroom[20]. By 1942 the sports day was held on a new cricket field off Trennick Lane. It was reported that 'the shape of the field makes it possible to set out a full Quarter-Mile track and a straight course for the 220 yards'. War conditions meant that there were no prizes as usual and boys ran 'only for the honour of gaining points for their respective houses'[21].

As the war progressed, activities outside of Treliske became more restricted due to the impossibilities of gaining transport. As a result, Treliske boys were frequently unable to attend services in the school chapel or to play away matches against other schools. The restrictions were not helped by outbreaks of childhood illnesses, such as German measles, which put the children into quarantine, though this did not prevent them helping to grow potatoes on the tennis court and front lawn which

Helping the war effort - digging for potatoes on the school field

had been ploughed up[22]. Hugh Berryman recalled that the boys had a rota to peel potatoes because there was a shortage of kitchen staff. In addition

every piece of available land was… ploughed to grow extra vegetables, it was suggested that the playing field at Treliske be planted but Mr T.S [Tommy Stratton] did not fancy ploughing up his cricket pitch. So it was agreed that the front lawn be used for this purpose. Much of the boys' spare time was spent planting and hoeing the crops and in fact there was a surplus which was sent to the main school[23].

Further impositions were prevented when in 1942

Military Authorities wished to requisition the Main Drive as a parking place for Lorries and also to put an Officers' Mess in the School. Fortunately, by negotiation between the Board of Education and the War Office, this plan …[was]…abandoned, so that the Preparatory School …[was]… able to carry on as before[24].

though some of the grounds were used as a military camp. Nor was it long before iron fencing was removed for munitions purposes. During the Spring term of 1940 there was one air raid alert and the boys ran inside and were told to sit along the corridor outside Mr Stratton's office. As a result, a working party from the main school dug a trench between the main lawn and the playing field during the summer of 1940. The governors' minutes recorded that 'no external shelters are proposed owing to the dangers of serious chills if boys were compelled to leave their beds to take refuge at night'. So although an external trench was dug for air raid protection at Treliske, it was only for daytime use; at night the central corridor of the main building would be used, because it was protected by thick granite. Charles Guest recalled that

I can't remember now if any shelters were ever actually erected in the trench. My memory fails me on that one. If I had to bet on it, I'd say not because it became part of our games to try jumping that trench long after the working party had left….[25].

School staff including Miss Parry, the school matron (left), Kitty Williams, the headmaster's secretary (behind) and Helena Stratton, who taught at Treliske (front centre)

However Hugh Berryman remembered running to an air raid shelter in the playing field; 'we prayed for this every night so we could get out of bed!'[26]

The main school had shelters in its main corridor, in the science block lecture theatre, and in the central corridors of Pentreve and Epworth. Kent College used the cellars at the Tremorvah Hotel and a purpose built shelter at Elstow[27]. By 1945 the school remained full, with applications exceeding the vacancies. The entrance examination would become more competitive, to follow the requirements laid down by the 1944 Education Act, leading to a higher standard of attainment. Similarly, entrance to the main school also depend-

Truro School and Kent College staff in 1944. Back row: S.H. Way, R.A. Day (K.C.), W.E.B. Worthington, Read, Thorpe, K. James, B. Williams (T.S. Bursar), Rev. Harris, A. Cubson (K.C.), S.A. Spicer (K.C.), Phillips. Front row: J.T. Hargreaves (K.C.), E.B. Willday, Miss Watson, Dr Magson, H.J. Prickett (K.C.), P.W. Richards (K.C.) C.F. Wilkes

ed on an entrance exam. As in the main school there were still staffing and equipment difficulties, but the 'lack of flannels and boots did not prevent cricket practices, and the House matches were played. But we were unable to secure any matches against teams from other schools…'[28].

The outbreak of war again led to a shortage of teaching staff as more and more were called up for service, which eventually made it most practical for Truro School and Kent College to merge together for the duration. By July 1942 twelve masters had joined the services and during the Speech Day service the headmaster stressed that they were not complaining at the lack of staff and teachers

as they realised that the war had to be won if they were to preserve their ideals of education, civilisation, and freedom, and it had to be won by young men. Sometimes they were inclined to grumble when some of their masters who were in the war were not being employed in a way of the greatest use to the nation. It was no use taking a man away from teaching Mathematics and relegating him to peeling potatoes[29].

Kent College junior school remained a totally separate entity based at the Tremorvah Hotel, rather than merging with Treliske, as the two senior schools had done.

Though the school magazine was much more restricted in size compared to the issues during the First World War, the activities and stationing of old boys was still mentioned and copies were sent to servicemen abroad.

Once again a roll of honour was created, with eventually more than 500 names on and the editorial frequently sent messages such as 'to our old boys we send our deepest affection, assuring them that, at all times and in all places, we are mindful of them; and to those on service our very best wishes for their welfare'[30]. Due to the lack of space in the school magazines there were only the briefest entries concerning old boys abroad, rather than letters being published as was the practise before.

Several old boys spent time as prisoners of war, including George Roynon, who was in the same camp as H. R. Taylor, a former art master. Roynon was captured when 'the Portugese boat on which he

A less formal photograph of Truro School staff

was sailing was stopped between St Vincent and Madeira by a German submarine and the 1st Officer was told to take all the ship's papers for examination. After half an hour the Officer was told to send back the ship's boat to fetch Mr Roynon. He was only permitted to bring one small hand bag. The ship was allowed to proceed, but the Captain was ordered not to use his wireless for 48 hours'[31]. Bertie Hamson and John Luke were taken prisoner by the Japanese and were interred in Hong Kong before later being moved to Stanley Camp.

There were a few lighter moments to break up the harshness of POW camp life:

Entertainment played a big part in keeping up morale. One summer evening we were having a show in the open. The Japanese sent a photographer to take pictures of the happy internees, but each, when developed, showed a sea of hands giving the 'V' sign! The Japanese stopped concerts for several months after that. Another

evening's entertainment was a ballet – 70 artistes dressed in mosquito net dresses, which had been dipped in triple dye, mercurochrome or some other colouring liquid, and flour bag costumes. It was one of the most spectacular shows I have ever seen. Rehearsals went on for months because people taking part were too weak for more than an hour's rehearsal a day[32].

Among the oldest old boys serving in the Forces was Leonard Bellingham, who had been at the school from 1908 to 1910. During the 1914-1918 war he had risen to be a major in the Wiltshire Regiment, and volunteered for service in the same regiment in 1940. He was taken prisoner and later died from wounds received in an air raid in 1943[33]. John St Aubyn Jewell had been at Truro School from 1884 to 1887 and served as a lieutenant on H.M.S. President until his death in May 1943 at the age of 67[34]. By 1948 there were 62 names on the memorial tablet, which was unveiled in the school

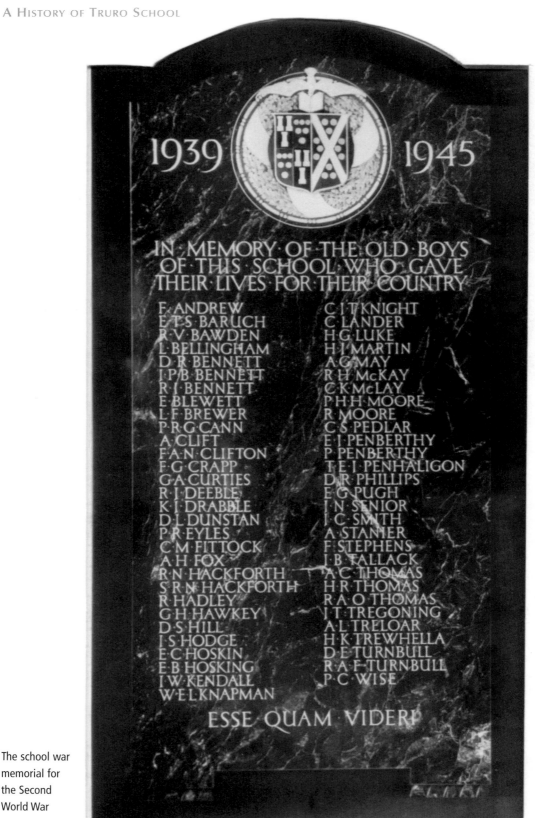

1939 1945

IN MEMORY OF THE OLD BOYS
OF THIS SCHOOL WHO GAVE
THEIR LIVES FOR THEIR COUNTRY

F ANDREW	C J T KNIGHT
E T S BARUCH	C LANDER
R V BAWDEN	H G LUKE
L BELLINGHAM	H J MARTIN
D R BENNETT	A G MAY
J P B BENNETT	R H McKAY
R J BENNETT	C K McLAY
E BLEWETT	P H H MOORE
L F BREWER	R MOORE
P R G CANN	C S PEDLAR
A CLIFT	E J PENBERTHY
F A N CLIFTON	P PENBERTHY
F G CRAPP	T E J PENHALIGON
G A CURTIES	D R PHILLIPS
R J DEEBLE	E G PUGH
K J DRABBLE	J N SENIOR
D L DUNSTAN	J C SMITH
P R EYLES	A STANIER
C M FITTOCK	F STEPHENS
A H FOX	J B TALLACK
R N HACKFORTH	A C THOMAS
S R N HACKFORTH	H R THOMAS
R HADLEY	R A O THOMAS
G H HAWKEY	J T TREGONING
D S HILL	A L TRELOAR
J S HODGE	H K TREWHELLA
E C HOSKIN	D E TURNBULL
E B HOSKING	R A F TURNBULL
J W KENDALL	P C WISE
W E L KNAPMAN	

ESSE QUAM VIDERI

The school war
memorial for
the Second
World War

Truro School and Kent College 1941 football team: Hosking, Morford (K.C.), Murch, Norris, Pawlyn, Hickson, Bryant, Black, Visick, Pascoe, Beasant (captain), Evans, McBride, Penrose

chapel. The tablet was designed by the Reverend G. Wynn of Newlyn, and made from green marble. However Jewell's name does not appear on it, nor does that of Edwin B. Martin, who worked in an R.A.F. factory in Gloucester, or that of Denis Donahue, who was a teacher at the school in 1941, and died while training for the R.A.F. in Canada. The memorial library, furbished from a fund raised by pupils and old boys, was opened on 19 July 1949.

As the war ended the school took stock of its position and started thinking of the future once more. The end of the war brought problems of its own, as society readjusted again; foreseen by Prickett, the headmaster of Kent College,

...the generation now coming into manhood was called by God to a task that was awful in its responsibility, yet glorious in its opportunity, but they could only fulfil that task if they recognised that evil was evil and know how to overcome it. There was a danger lest in their enthusiasm to win the war they blurred the moral

issue and called evil good and good evil. ...Unless they were determined to fight against unemployment, poverty, and all kinds of social injustice after the war, those evils would surely return in a worse form than they had ever known. They had accepted ... the curtailment of their comforts and the control of private interests for the winning of the war, and they must prepare to face the problems of peace in the same spirit[35].

Malvern Lodge was purchased in 1944 as an extra boarding house, its garden adjoined that of Pentreve[36], and Treliske was reorganised so it gained an assembly hall and a science and nature study laboratory. In 1947 the first resident chaplain was taken on at the school with the appointment of the Reverend N. Richardson.

In 1946 Magson retired as headmaster, having stayed on an extra year while the war lasted. 'Dr Magson had made character building as well as scholastic achievement his aims in furthering the development of the School'[37]. His place was filled

Above - The first boarders at Malvern Lodge in the summer of 1946. Back row (left to right): J.E. Kerkin, K.J.O. Goddard, Mr and Mrs Worthington, L.J. Penna, D.A. Jones, J.C. Mann. Seated: I Sleeman, C.G. Symons, H.D. Richards, R.T. Jelbert, H.T. Bruce, P.B. Hutchings, J.O. Nash. Front row: T.T. Dignan, R.M. Williams, H. Berryman
Below - Malvern Lodge

by Albert Lowry Creed, previously headmaster at Staveley Grammar School in Derbyshire[38].

The Local Education Authority recognised the School's wish to serve the community and according to the 1944 Education Act it was possible for parents to receive financial help if they wished to send their sons as boarders, though it appeared rather slow to be implemented. At the 1946 Speech Day, Colonel Smith, chairman of the governors', intimated that 'the special character of the school would be retained even if it involved a reduction or loss of government grant'[39].

The school scout group was revived in 1945, though this time it was called the 3rd Truro Troop, bringing with it its own magazine, *Ascent*. Toc H, was revived and among the first meetings included a talk by Winston Graham on 'my job as a novelist'. The A.T.C. continued with a 'startling' rise in numbers, while new clubs were started, including boxing, gardening, Young Farmers' and the 'Q' Society, interested in the arts. Similarly older clubs were restarted, such as chess matches against other teams. Camps, day trips and travel abroad were also resumed.

Before they left, in September 1945, Kent College presented a cup to Truro School, which was used for school athletics, an area of sport in which they had been quite prominent while staying in Truro. The sporting life of the school slowly got back to pre-war standards, with the number of football teams increasing. The memorial pavilion was dismantled in 1947 and moved from field 7 to overlook fields 1 and 2 because the original memorial field was sold off after 20 acres of fields were bought nearer the school. House jerseys were introduced, either green, red, dark blue or light blue for each of the houses; school colours were now only to be worn in representative matches. Team colours also changed slightly, being awarded only to those with a definite place in the school team.

There was also sporting success among the old boys. In 1948 J. Kendall Carpenter became the first old boy to gain a varsity rugby blue.

Punishments at Treliske in the 1940s. From an article by C. Guest in the Truro School Former Pupils Association Newsletter, February 2001.

The ruler: for minor infractions, 5 across the knuckles. 'The ruler was never lifted very high, caused no damage and hurt enough to make you not want to offend again and to keep on your toes.
The slipper: for more serious offences, but not as serious as those which justified a caning. Applied across the buttocks.

The cane: for serious offences not warranting expulsion, applied across the buttocks.

Weeds: a summer punishment for minor infractions, but effective. Involved lifting 50 or 100 weeds by the roots out of the cricket pitch.

Lines: for minor infractions. 'There were special lines books, with Grange covers…and lines printed across the pages in sets of four parallels – two thick lines with a thinner line above and below'.
In the main school the slipper, ruler and weeds were not used as punishments, but lines and the cane were.
Prefects could give lines as well as masters. Corporal punishment only administered by the Headmaster and Second Master.

Peter Watkins (1935-39) entered the Royal Engineers Technical School at 16 and was subsequently commissioned in India. Recalling his memories from his service for the former pupils' newsletter, new light was thrown on 'Truro School as a preparation for military service':I bumped into three Old Boys during my service in Burma, Malaya and the Dutch East Indies (now Indonesia). They were all Senior Officers and all had one thing in common apart from being Old Boys – they had all been expelled! Honestly! Which I suppose does show a certain flair for initiative, which no doubt contributed to their rapid promotions. However expulsion from Truro School is not, I believe, essential to success in later life!

Albert Lowry Creed, the fifth headmaster

A.L. Creed (1946 – 1959)

In December 1945 it was announced that Dr Magson would be retiring at the end of the 1946 spring term. His place would be taken by A.L. Creed, at that time the headmaster of Staveley Grammar School in Derbyshire, a mixed school of about 400 boys and girls. Creed was the son of the Reverend A.H. Creed, a Methodist minister whose circuits were in the north of England. His mother was the daughter of the Reverend F.M. Lowry, who was well known in Cornwall.

Creed was educated at Kingswood School from 1920 to 1928, where he was known for his 'courtesy, kindness and gentleness …with a distinguished track record both in the classroom, on the games field and as a head of house'[1]. He won a scholarship to Downing College, Cambridge, where he took the Natural Science Tripos and specialised in biology. After attaining his teaching qualification he worked at Stretford Grammar School and Bishop's Stortford College, and from 1939 to 1942 he was housemaster at Christ's Hospital[2]. Under his headmastership Truro School expanded in many ways,

with new buildings and facilities, and changes to the curriculum. 'Mr Creed stressed the importance of the right balance between academic, physical, recreative and spiritual training, if a liberal education, training for leadership and good citizenship and the development of sound character were to be fostered in the school…'[3]. He left Truro in 1959 to take up the position of headmaster at Kingswood School; was headmaster there from 1959 to 1970. He became vice-president of the Methodist conference in 1961[4]. While in Cornwall he became well known as a Methodist local preacher and was also the chairman of the West Cornwall Hospital Management Committee.

After retiring from Kingswood School, Creed went to Botswana for a year with his wife as volunteer teachers. Mrs Creed taught English in a school in Gabarone, while Mr Creed did administration work in the Education Department as well as some teaching[5]. They later returned to England to live at Chapel-en-Frith near Stockport.

Extracts from the School Rules of the 1950s

Bounds and Exeats

All boys will keep off the lawns and flower beds.

Day boys who stay to school lunch (other than prefects) must obtain permission from the master on duty if they need to go into the city between 12.35 and 1.55pm.

Boys may not boat at Malpas on Sundays, and may not use Malpas Road on Sunday afternoons without permission.

Boys may go for walks within the area bounded by Trafalgar Square, Malpas Road, Tresillian and the London Road.

Sixth form boarders may have bicycles at school. These must be kept in the cycle shed (charge 2/6). All bicycles must be clearly marked to indicate the name of the owner. They must not be ridden down the hill and must not be mounted before the junction of Trennick Lane and St Clement's Hill…

Unless specific permission has been obtained no boarder who is not a prefect may visit the cinema.

No boy may enter a public house, take alcoholic drinks, smoke, or take part in any form of gambling either during term time or with an official school party during the holidays.

Games Rules

Indoor house shoes must not be worn on the school fields.

Miscellaneous

Transistor radios may not be used between 9am and 4pm (1pm on Wednesdays and Saturdays), between tea and chapel on Sunday evenings, and during Communion Services.

No card games are to be played before 4pm on Mondays, Tuesdays, Thursdays and Fridays (1pm on Wednesdays and Saturdays).

Running is not permitted in any of the school corridors. All boys must keep to the left.

No boarder may buy a Sunday newspaper without his housemaster's permission.

Boys should raise their caps to members of staff. They should stand when the headmaster or a visitor enters a room.

Boys will at all times be polite to all people.

No boys may drive a car to school unless his parents have written to the headmaster and obtained his agreement.

No boy may ride in a car driven by another boy or by an old boy under 25 years old unless a special agreement has been made.

All breakages of school property must be reported immediately to the member of staff responsible and to the Breakages Prefect.

1950-1959

Above - E.B. Willday opening new classrooms, 1953
Opposite page - The 1950 School tennis team. Standing: B.H.T Wearne, K.J. Keast, S.G Heyworth. Sitting: R.N. Curnow, F.J. Exelby (captain), M.A. Bourdeaux

1950 – 1959: Moving On

The 1950s was a welcome period of calm compared to the previous decade, though building work had resumed as the school continued to expand and by the end of the decade the number of pupils was double what it had been 20 years previously. Boarding was still a popular choice, leading to the expansion of the boarding facilities and after school activities, which were still generally aimed at boarders rather than day boys. By the early 1950s the number of boys taking the School Certificate was reduced because an age limit of 16 was applied, and the Advanced and Ordinary Level General Certificates in Education were being introduced. It was planned that 'in future years they would gradually reduce the number of subjects to be taken at the ordinary level by those boys who would be taking subjects at the advanced and scholarship levels'.

A-levels included a general paper covering English language, literature, art, music and current affairs, as well as general topics in science and current affairs. The fourth and fifth form choices were expanding, with the inclusion of an agricultural course which would meet the needs of certain boys who might come from an agricultural background, and who intended to take up agriculture or horticulture without any training at a college'[1]. There was also a growing proportion of the sixth form who went on to attend university or training college. Steps towards alleviating the ongoing demand for a wider secondary educational choice for boys in Truro were finally taken with the opening of Penweathers School, a secondary modern school, in September 1958[2].

The expansion of the school continued with the building of new classrooms and improved facilities for science, opened in 1953 by Mr Willday, to mark his long service to the school. By 1953 Malvern boarding house had been in use for several years, though it was not until September 1952 that the whole building, incorporating the flats in Hillside and Kilbryde, became fully operational. Poltisco

Above - The school swimming pool opened in May 1954.
Before it was built the school held swimming lessons at
Loe Beach
Right - The school rugby sevens team at Rosslyn Park

was opened in 1954, initially with 17 boarders from the lower school, and the first forms were taught in huts in the grounds[3]. From 1879 to 1920 Poltisco had been owned by George Dixon, who lived there with his wife and their seven children. His daughter Nellie, writing in the 1950s, described Poltisco as lying in a narrow rectangle of land rising steeply from the river level to the hill top, providing an appropriate area equating to '3 acres and a cow'. The west-facing house was built circa 1820, and later features included a croquet and tennis lawn. Tales of her childhood included the recollection of the Implacable, an old French ship captured by Nelson and laid up near the King Harry Passage[4].

A swimming pool was finally built at the school, so that the swimming lessons were no longer held at

Loe Beach. The open-air pool was opened in May 1954, by Mr P.M. Williams of Burncoose, though it was not actually finished until Whitsun[5]. Swimming at Loe Beach had been re-established after the war in 1950, after previously being held at Malpas or the city baths. 'The early events passed quite pleasantly, the connoisseurs were much intrigued by a certain Wickett competitor's Right Arm only stroke, and by

Poltisco House, which was acquired for school boarding accommodation in 1954.

the goggles and bathing caps affected by the swimmers'[6]. The new pool at the school meant that swimming, as well as life saving.

Rugby was becoming ever more popular again, so much so that by 1960 it was played more than football. In 1951 a group of 21 boys travelled to Twickenham to watch John Kendall-Carpenter captain the English rugby team against France. In 1952 a rugby team from Truro School attended the Sevens competition at Rosslyn Park, and got through to the last sixteen where they were beaten by Christ's Hospital[7]. Consequent trips to Rosslyn Park had less success, only getting through to the second round. A successful rugby tour was also taken to Germany, playing against teams in Hanover and winning all four matches. The trip became 'the most moving expression of international goodwill that anyone could experience', as participants saw how Hanover had been rebuilt after the war[8]. Cricket and tennis tournaments were played during the holidays and on a more sedate level, chess continued to be popular, with matches played against different schools.

Extra-curricular activities continued to flourish. Mock general elections were frequently held, and were just as frequently won by conservatives, fending off the liberal, nationalist and radical candidates. The Debating Society discussed various topical subjects including National Service, the colonial policy in Africa, the need for educational reform and the good or bad use of television. Similarly the History Society discussed topical subjects including the Suez crisis, which was enlivened 'by the helpful willingness of a certain Socialist gentleman to argue with anyone, especially our chairman, about anything'[9].

There was a proliferation of new groups, including the carol society, the surveying club, the gardening club and the model aircraft club. The Young Farmers' Club, raising various chickens, goats and pigs, morphed into the Agricultural Society, while the photography club was revived and marked by the renovation of the dark room. The Electronics Society was formed by Mr Scales to instil new life into the radio club, which led to working on a hi-fi amplifier, a television receiver and a Geiger tube, as

The 1950s chess team

well as the construction of one-valve and multi-valve radios[10]. The Scouts expanded to include a Malvern and Pentreve troop and an additional Sea Scouts troop was formed.

Like the main school, Treliske was increasing in size with 39 day boys and 50 boarders by the mid 1950s. Renovations were taking place here too, with a new dining room and dormitory built, and Mr and Mrs Stratton moved into the new housemaster's accommodation[11]. An open-air pool was also built at Treliske, encouraging swimming among the juniors. Similarly the football team was steadily improving, now able to play against other schools including Bosvigo and Mount Charles, since the war had finished and rationing of petrol eased. Some of the comments made about players were reminiscent of those made decades earlier about the main school team.

Penhaligon* was the outstanding player of the term and apart from the lethargic Burroughs and the lively but diminutive Kent, the only member of the team who had any ball control. Although goalkeeper Davies showed a strange reluctance to use his hands, he was generally safe in his unorthodox way. Opie was a useful back and Pester a supreme trier, with the utmost determination, but as yet an inability to distribute the ball. Collins did some useful things but was generally slow to turn. Of the halves, Harvey impressed as a player who can see the value of first-time kicking in defence. Kent may one day be a very fine footballer[12].

(*David Penhaligon, later Liberal M.P. for Truro)

The 3rd Truro, Truro School, Scout Troop c.1956

In addition to rugby tours to London, Taunton and Germany, several other countries were visited and while on a trip to Norway in 1950, Mr Rhead took 'on everyone else in a genuine snowball fight and fared rather badly'[13]. There were several cycling trips, including around Denmark in 1955 and a particularly memorable cycling tour two years, from Bath to Ely. After overcoming a snow shower in April 'it was on this run that one, who is to be nameless, went plunging down a 1 in 5 hill, with a hairpin bend at the bottom. At the peak of speed he found he was brakeless, and hit a limestone hedge. The frame of his bike was set at an angle of 165° for the rest of the journey'[14]. Trips were not limited to the main school: Treliske visited the Netherlands that same Easter, making the flight over in a Viscount which 'was a pleasant welcome to

Holland'. While there, the group visited Arnhem, Delft and The Hague, and watched an opera by Strauss[15].

The main alteration to the school magazine at this time was the introduction of *Terraces*, a separate literary section, designed to encourage and incorporate more pupils' work. In 1958 a magazine competition was launched between forms, in which entrants had to publish three editions. Marks were awarded for poetry, feature articles, news and the magazine's presentation: the first final was won by Form 3A[16].

The Old Boys' Association branches expanded in number during the 1950s, with new ones in Plymouth, Lancashire and Birmingham and proposed meetings in Bristol. The various association activities were fully resumed after the

Above - Gathering for the Old Boys' Association dinner outside the school c.1955

Bottom left - Menu card for the 75th anniversary dinner arranged by the newly formed Truro School Society, held at the school. Bottom right - Service programme to celebrate the school's 75th anniversary

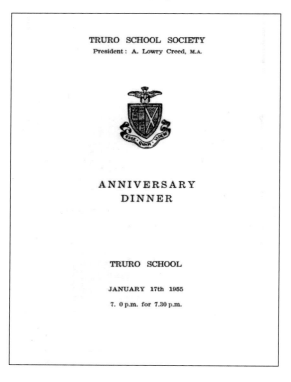

TRURO SCHOOL SOCIETY
President: A. Lowry Creed, M.A.

ANNIVERSARY
DINNER

TRURO SCHOOL

JANUARY 17th 1955

7. 0 p.m. for 7.30 p.m.

TRURO SCHOOL
—
Seventy-fifth Anniversary
1880 - 1955

May 26th, 1955

The woodwork room, converted from the A.T.C. hut in the 1940s and later moved to where the sixth form centre now stands

war, including motor runs along the south coast and the north coast, from Portreath to Carbis Bay[17].

The Truro School Society was established in July 1953 to bring together staff, governors, parents and former pupils[18]. 'These meetings provided an admirable opportunity for discussion of educational topics especially in relation to the School and also enabled people to enjoy many social functions – not least those summer evening motor runs through the Cornish countryside to places of interest and a pasty'[19].

In 1955 the school celebrated its 75th anniversary, holding several functions to celebrate the occasion. The newly formed Truro School Society hosted a dinner with Sir Archie Marshall Q.C. as the guest speaker, who remarked that the school buildings were much changed since his time there

between 1911 and 1917. Creed calculated that in the previous 75 years, fifteen generations of boys had passed through the school and it had expanded considerably from the original 35 pupils to 535. Similarly the land the school occupied had increased from the original five acres to 55[20]. On 26 May a short service was held to celebrate the anniversary, followed by a mock general election after which the boys were taken on excursions to various parts of the county, such as Polperro, Land's End, Fowey, St Mawes and Bodmin Moor. On their return to school there was a birthday tea and a film show[21].

During the summer term of 1959, Creed announced his intention of leaving Truro School, to take up the position of headmaster at Kingswood School, his alma mater. Under Creed's

Teaching staff from the 1950s

headmastership the number of pupils in the school had almost doubled, the curriculum had been extended and the facilities available had increased: the headmaster's influence showing everywhere in the expansion. The dormitories were renamed Hall, Trennick and Tower and given their own housemasters, similar to the other boarding houses. The school had progressed far since Creed's early days, which had been governed by the rationing of food and petrol and the need to face the problems, as well as the opportunities that resulted from the 1939 - 1945 War[22].

1959 also saw the close of an earlier era with the death of Howard Chennalls, at the age of 92. He was the last survivor of the school's very first intake of pupils 1880.

Westminster Training College alumni who became Truro School teachers. Westminster was a Methodist teacher training college, originally based in London but later moved to Oxford in the 1950s.

George Jervis, Noel Horley, Sam Melling, Tommy Stratton, Alan Ayres, Sam Rhead, Barry Worthington, Alan Scales, Tony Aldwinkle, Allan Church, Brian Jackson, Alan Monks, E.H. Magson and Bert Willday.

From a 1950s Prospectus
General Domestic Arrangements
Health

The general health of the School has been excellent. This due not only to the healthy position of the School, but to the care and attention given to each boy individually. The Matron and her Assistant Matron are in charge of the Dispensary and Sick Room, and minor health disorders are quickly remedied. Any case of infectious illness is immediately isolated. Records are kept of height and weight, and cases of too rapid or too slow development are quickly detected. The Sick Bay has two wards and an observation room, together with its own kitchen and bathroom and a day room for convalescents. The School is conveniently near to the Royal Cornwall Infirmary and the School Medical Officer visits the School daily.

Dietary

Special care has been taken with the domestic arrangements. The kitchens have modern equipment and are under the control of a qualified Caterer. In order to avoid monotony, there is no formal weekly dietary, and the scheme of meals is drawn up to cover as long a period as possible.
All milk is from a Tuberculin Tested herd.
Breakfast is served at 8.0 (Sundays, 8.30); Dinner at 12.45 (Sundays, 1); Tea at 5.30 and Supper at 8. All boys have milk daily. It is particularly requested that tuck parcels should not be sent too frequently. A school tuck-shop is organised by the masters. All profits are devoted to the Sports' Fund.

Pocket Money

Boys should not be supplied too liberally with pocket money. Arrangements can be made for a weekly sum to be handed to each boy and charged on the bill. It is suggested that this be 2s.0d. for boys under 13. 3s.0d. for boys aged 13-15 and not more than 4s.6d. for boys over the age of 15. This might be supplemented by a sum in deposit say from 15s. to £1.5s.

1960-1969

1960 – 1969: A School for all Seasons

The retirement of Bert Willday in 1960 marked the end of another era, since he had been at the school for almost forty years. He had provided a certain stability during times of upheaval and change, teaching English and History, and becoming known as the school's very own 'Mr Chips'. He was an outstanding and enthusiastic sportsman, playing in the early years and later coaching the school teams. He played centre-half, and later goalkeeper, for the school 'club' team, which was partly made up of staff so they could play other local teams. He was sports master until 1947: in recording his achievements, the school magazine of July 1960 recalled 'his personal skill in games and his wise instruction laid the foundation for the high reputation for cricket and football that Truro School holds today in the Westcountry'[1]. In 1913 he had attended Westminster Training College where his tutor was E.H. Magson. In 1915 he joined the Royal Artillery and while in France was taken prisoner, spending the rest of the war working as a blacksmith in a German P.O.W. camp. Tom Magson recalled:

He had been one of my father's best students at Westminster before the war, and returned from P.O.W. camp weighing little more than 6 stone. In 1921, when my father took over the school, the staff was almost non-existent. He invited Bert to be second master. For several years he was a very sick man indeed – but such an outstanding teacher and leader, that his frequent illness did not seem to affect his pupils[2].

Willday became good friends with the parents of Alan Pownell, a friend of Tom Magson's, and married their daughter Brownie[3]. Overleigh was built for his accommodation after he married[4]. He was 'never known to raise his voice. Such respect as he commanded can never be cultivated; it emanated from the integrity in the depths of his own personality'. He oversaw many aspects of school life, was involved in the early school plays and instigated the Masters' Feast held at the end of each autumn term. In discussions between the headmaster and the

Page 137: E.B. Willday, Second Master 1921 – 1960

second master, where new ideas were raised, Magson often found it difficult to remember which part of a scheme belonged to whom. He was also known for a dry sense of humour, J. Bedford Daniel recalled being told 'Daniel, laddie, one little thing to remember when fielding – always pick up the ball before you throw it'[5].

W.E.B. Worthington, a former old boy of Kent College, who had been at Truro since 1941, was appointed second master after Willday retired and he held that position until 1968[6]. In 1961, Stratton retired from Treliske and his position as housemaster was taken by A.W. Ayres. Tommy Stratton had come to the school in 1927, and after marrying Helena Rowe, a headmistress in her own right, took charge of the junior boys at Pentreve, later becoming the head of the prep school at Treliske after much persuasion[7]. In 1963 'Sammy' Way, music master, also retired after for forty years.

In 1965 the school magazine announced the

Ken James, 'the embodiment of rugby at Truro School' (right) and John Kendall-Carpenter, former pupil and England rugby player, photographed in 1980

marriage of an English Teacher, Brian Drury, to the school housekeeper Miss Macdonald, which was to be the first wedding held in the school chapel[8].

Several aspects of school life changed over the decade. There was an increased emphasis on choosing careers and senior boys were offered an introduction to industry. In addition old boys were invited to give talks on different types of employment. The traditional speech day became an open day for the school and the 'hour long speeches in St Mary's entered the history books'. Open day involved numerous displays and exhibitions, music recitals and a sixth-form forum. A compromise was made that if there was 'a public outcry' at this change then the school would revert to the old-style speech day. At the time the new open day appeared to be received favourably[9], but this did not last, and it reverted back to the more formal speech day before long.

Building work continued at the school, occasionally causing disruption to normal school life. The chapel, frequently used for assemblies, plays, lectures and music lessons, was closed in the early 1960s for structural repair. The gym above was also affected and gymnastic activities would take place outside if the weather permitted. With the gym out of use, Trennick dormitory was used for 'O' level exams and 'the usual occupants slept in the most unusual places'[10]. A new organ was installed in the chapel; a 'two-manual tracker' organ from Bideford, to replace the Aeolean Chamber organ that had been in the school for 40 years and had become affected by the damp and impossible to tune[11]. The opening of the Graham Smith rooms marked the retirement of the chairman of the school governors, Graham Burrell Smith; he was the last of his family to be on the board of governors, which had been connected with the school since its foundation.

The school band in 1961, after achieving success in the Cornwall Music Festival

Graham Smith opened the new building was opened on 10 September 1966, using a golden key presented to his aunt, Lady Smith, after she opened the school chapel in 1928[12].

Rugby had taken over from football as the most dominant sport in the school, a trend that began after the Second World War, keenly supported by Ken James who was described as the embodiment of rugby at Truro School[13]. Football was mainly played by the lower years in the school, though in 1967 the first reports of the 1st and 2nd XI soccer teams since the 1940s were printed in the school magazine. The 1st XI won four matches, drew three and lost one[14]. Cricket continued with a full season, including the annual match between Truro and Kent College. Tennis and swimming were continued with enthusiasm started and a prefects' hockey team was established. Other new sports

were introduced to the school in this decade. A golf society was formed in 1961 by sixth formers, who practised on the school fields as well as at Truro Golf Club[15].

General nautical interest was sparked and maintained by the Ship Society, which included trips to Falmouth Docks and Penzance among its activities. This enthusiasm for boats led to a more practical interest and a sailing club was formed a few years later. The sailing took place on the River Fal and Peter Lang was nominated commodore of the club. In July 1968 a Truro School team took part in the Public Schools Firefly Championships at Itchenor, where the Firefly was first built. In the first race the team finished second behind the eventual winners, Sevenoaks School. By the end of the second day they were 9th overall and eventually finished in 13th place[16].

Above - Marching through town to Boscawen Bridge for the Caps Ceremony

Below - Caps Ceremony: a school tradition that has passed into history. School leavers threw their mortar boards from Boscawen Bridge into the river on the last Sunday of the summer term

Cross-country running gained a new lease of life in the mid 1960s: a 'sport of mud, hills, water, mud, and even more mud', generally around a circuit that included Pencalenick and Malpas. Continuing the theme of mud and fresh air, the Duke of Edinburgh Award scheme became more popular at the school, leading to the senior scout group being disbanded in 1963, because several scouts were undertaking the Award instead. The following year the first boys from Truro School were participating in the Gold Award while at the same time competing in the Ten Tors Challenge on Dartmoor[17]. The Ten Tors team in 1965 were more successful than the previous year, overcoming map reading errors on the first day to complete more than half the 50-mile course by the evening and finishing the next day with an hour to spare[18]. Indoor activities included a gym club, for which Mr Lang made a trampoline, rock climbing and a table tennis club, which quickly became quite successful[19].

The first skiing trip to the Swiss Alps, which was to become a regular occurrence, was noted for several mishaps, some of which were possibly self-inflicted. One boy took part in 'ski-borne' aerobatics', which resulted in a broken leg and on the return journey from a visit to Liechtenstein, 'we were almost shot at by the Swiss Army at the frontier, who for some reason or another seemed to resent our presence. We were also sworn at by a group of Italian workmen who were widening the road. From these encounters we gathered that Italian workmen do not enjoy being called 'tagliatelli', etc'[20].

Drama took a break from tradition at this time, including girls in the production of school plays. The film unit, a branch of the photography society, began making home movies and included a mixed cast, with girls from Truro County Grammar School[21]. A few years later the grammar school girls were also involved in Truro School's production of George Bernard Shaw's *Arms and the Man*. A review

Borlase Society membership card; the society was for the enthusiasts of archaeology and Cornish history

of the play commented that 'a young boy, playing a female role, is never completely convincing and has an unduly heavy burden on his shoulders'[22], reflecting an enthusiasm for the change in policy. *An Italian Straw Hat*, performed in 1969, was a joint production with Truro High School, and brought exclamations of 'at last a play where the girls really were girls! Gone the judiciously placed football socks and dusters, gone too the garters and string of desperate attempts to keep them up...'[23].

As ever, there was a proliferation of other societies and activities. Charity fundraising raised money for nutritional food for Kenyans in the 'War on Want' appeal and Treliske raised funds for the 'Milk for Madras' appeal in 1969, to send dried milk to India[24]. The Y.F.C. at Truro School continued to grow vegetables and raise a variety of animals - on one occasion taking part in a cockroach 'grand national' at Threemilestone. There also seemed to be a growing zoo at Treliske, with a variety of pets being looked after, including fourteen budgerigars, five guinea-pigs, thirteen pigeons, one hamster and one rabbit[25].

A junior 'Q' society was started to introduce the arts to the junior forms; it included a wide range of topics including painting, Turkish village life, make-up, corporal punishment, photography and music. The meetings took the form of debates, mock radio programmes, films, talks and quizzes[26].

The archaeological society was renamed the Borlase society in 1963, and had talks on the neo-bronze age settlements at Gwithian and the life and work of William Borlase, the eighteenth-century antiquarian[27]. The long standing debating society continued with discussions on a variety of topical issues, including the motions that children's reading should be controlled and that Carnaby Street was a 'cancer' in society – both were defeated[28]. The electronics society developed a communication system, which was used at the 1960 sports day[29].

Among the more serious clubs, such as those for

Caps Ceremony on Boscawen Bridge in 1963. Soon after this tradition ceased when the bridge was replaced by Morlaix Avenue

angling, motor enthusiasts, campanology and the film unit, there were also those which appear to be less serious, such as the Sockiety, which aimed to put a pink sock on top of Everest, and the secret 'Z' society which folded in 1966 when it officially wound up 'and will not require rewinding for another seven years. The rewinding ceremony was poorly attended, no doubt because the need for secrecy prevented the Head Bard from informing any of the members that the ceremony was to take place'[30].

The appeal of the musical societies varied. The choir was still popular, with separate groups for day-boys and boarders. Annual trips to the Isles of Scilly were arranged for the choir to give recitals;

they arrived in St Mary's with 'fishing rods, sleeping bags and infallible sun-tan oil for ten days of sunning, swimming and singing, based at the Methodist Church Hall' and left with sunburn and many 'unforgettable' memories[31]. In contrast the orchestra was very small, making 'a fighting come-back' from obscurity with five violins, two clarinets and a recorder[32]. A jazz appreciation society and folk music club were started as was the 'M' Society 'for the musical elite' which was accused of 'trying to out 'Q' the 'Q' Society'[33].

The school magazine, like the other areas of school life, saw change once again. The page size increased and students' artwork was included. Adverts were introduced from sources that were

Above - View of the school from the river at Boscawen Bridge
Below - The athletics field, built in the mid 1950s: now mostly tarmaced over and used for sport, games and car parking

The dining room and dining staff

considered appropriate, such as Harrods and Midland Bank, as well as those for local businesses like the Red Lion Hotel in Truro. The change was necessary because the magazine had been produced at a loss for the previous several years and it was necessary to make it more profitable[34]. The Terraces section continued with various literary and poetic pieces, including a report on the revived tale of Jimsky the school ghost[35]. The next change to the magazine would come in 1970, when it became an annual publication instead of every term. A form newssheet competition was established in 1963, though only a few classes entered. Among the entries, Form 1a received comment for spending too much time reporting on rugby and the Beatles. At the same time Form 4 of Treliske was producing a fortnightly newsletter called the *Treliske Times*[36].

The Old Boys' Association formed closer links with the London Cornish rugby club during the 1960s, which reflected the large number of pupils who had moved away from Cornwall to work and study. London Cornish held its 80th anniversary dinner and several former pupils were on the committee; Sir Archie Marshall QC held the presidency, C.C. Bennett was the chairman and A.D. Nicholls chaired the dinner committee. At the dinner, the toast to the county and London Cornish was proposed by the headmaster, Derek Burrell[37].

The inaugural dinner of the Midland Old Boys' branch was held in Birmingham in 1960[38]. In 1969 Robert Shaw attended the Old Boys' dinner at the Savoy Hotel, Newquay, as guest of honour, just as the film *A Man for all Seasons*, in which he played Henry VIII, was showing in Truro. He recalled that 'many people at Truro School, including the late Dr E.H. Magson, who was then the headmaster, were wonderful to me. When I went on later to the acting school, I could not feel quite the same debt to the teachers there as I did to the staff of Truro School'[39].

D.W. Burrell, the sixth headmaster

D.W. Burrell (1925 - 1999)

In his own words Derek Burrell was born and raised 'halfway between Spurs and Arsenal Football Ground', being educated at Tottenham Grammar School, and later studied English and History at Queen's College, Cambridge, where he was secretary of the Cambridge United Christian Council and a group leader in the Methodist Society[1]. Before coming to Truro School in 1959 he taught at Solihull School and Dollar Academy, Dunblane. He held the position of Vice-President of the Methodist Conference from 1987 to 1988.

When he first took on the headmastership of Truro School in 1959, there were only two schools in Cornwall that continued as Wesleyan establishments: Truro and the West Cornwall School for Girls in Penzance, which closed in the late 1960s. The fate of the Penzance school 'suggested to some that Truro School might well go into the state system to secure its future in this remote area of the Realm'[2]; instead it became fully independent following its status as a direct grant school. Burrell wrote 'there are, of course, critics who believe that Methodism has no right to run independent fee paying schools, branded as elitist, privileged and divisive'[3]. This view was long-standing and arose in 1880 when some thought the foundation of the school in Cornwall was part of a wider 'demonstration of Methodist strength in the face of the creation of the Truro Diocese. Some think it was the other way around'[4].

By the time Burrell retired in 1986, Truro School had become co-educational in the sixth form and had continued to increase its size and facilities. As a headmaster he was '...most approachable ... knowing everyone and caring especially for the strugglers and those in trouble, bringing a simple humanity into the heart of the school...'[5]. His out of school activities included acting as vice-chairman of Luton Industrial College, participating as a member of the B.B.C.'s regional Religious Advisory Council, the South West Council of the Christian Education Movement and the local committee of N.C.H. Action for Children, as well as being on

D.W. Burrell in the 1980 Centenary Booklet

In the words of Lorenz Hart 'if you asked me I could write a book'. Tales could be told of teachers who went just in time and of pupils who outstayed their welcome. Tales could be told of teachers who were here just a couple of years and who we remember with affection … and of pupils who were here seven years or more and whom some of us would pass in the street now and not recognise. Tales could be told of boys who left under a quiet cloud, and of others whom teachers here nearly three decades look back on as the greats (they don't make 'em like that nowadays). But I will mention my deputies as representatives of the many colleagues who have worked with me since 1959. Bert Willday has been praised…He saw me in, as it were. Barry Worthington was the Second Master for most of the Sixties. His explosive hearty, staccato and distinctive laugh, and his looks of amazed incredulity are with me for good. Cyril Wilkes stood in when Barry was ill, as he often was, and it was a happy triumvirate that we became in due course. There was no doubt that when Barry died Cyril should succeed. The loud laugh was replaced by the stifled snort and satirical smile. But those distinctive sounds and reassuring looks are gone … It is a truism that the deputy headmaster runs the school. Any success the school enjoys now is largely theirs, and any reputation it enjoys, due to the boys they educated.

several other Methodist and educational committees. He was appointed Deputy Lieutenant of Cornwall in 1993. Burrell also became a popular and respected preacher; 'his life was marked by his thorough commitment to Christ and a love for his Church and its heritage in John Wesley, but his was no narrow piety…'[6].

1970-1979

Girls from Truro High School in the Friday woodwork class. Boys from Truro School went to the High School on Fridays to learn subjects such as home economics

1970 - 1979:
The Beginning of Full Independence

The 1970s witnessed various changes in educational policy, which created some concern for Truro School, especially in the early part of the decade. The changes had begun in 1965 when the government declared that secondary education should be reorganised along comprehensive school lines. This would include the abolition of the eleven plus and 'all children would be in the same school after eleven, as they had been in the same school before'[1]. In addition the closure of the West Cornwall School in Penzance and the selling off of its buildings in 1969 caused repercussions for Truro School[2].

By this time there was also a revival in the belief that the Methodist Conference should not own a public school because it was seen as elitist; though in many ways the school had changed little from its original intentions - grant aided places allowed a wider range of pupils to attend the school. The headmaster Derek Burrell foresaw that 'developments in National and Cornish Education mean that Truro School cannot go on as it has done for the last thirty or forty years', and that within ten to fifteen years it would be a different school again. Direct Grant schools were to be closed nationally,

Building the sports hall and technology block, a 'D.I.Y.' project directed by Dennis Keam, the technology master, and carried out by pupils, staff, old boys and parents as well as contractors

which meant that Truro School would have to increase fees to compensate or become increasingly reliant on state funding and less independent[3].

Speculation and concern intensified in 1972 when the Methodist education authority announced that it was willing to sell Truro School[4]. In order to fulfil its objectives the County Council were looking to establish two comprehensive schools in Truro, one on the west side and another on the east side of the city. It was proposed that the Council buy the buildings of Truro School to create one of the comprehensive schools, because there had been a decline in numbers at the school and boarders were there was a hostile meeting in October, in which calls were made for governors to resign. The following February the Cornwall Education Committee decided against buying the school buildings.

Bedford Daniel was appointed the new chairman of the governors in 1973. The '...reorganisation was bound to be complicated because of the existence of the two direct-grant schools.... associated with the County. It was inevitable that the County could not go Comprehensive and continue to send selected academics to a direct-grant school'[5]. Consequently it appeared increasingly likely that Truro School, along with Truro High School, would become fully independent when the government phased out direct grant status, which eventually occurred in 1977[6]. Burrell was somewhat regretful that the school had become fully independent because the direct-grant had 'bridged the state provision of education (right for the majority) and the independent area (likely to persist in a free society)'[7]. The new state comprehensives, Richard Lander and Penair, were finally opened in September 1979.

The next fundamental change to the school was the admittance of girls to the sixth form in 1976. This was the first step towards coeducation and by widening the school's appeal it helped to redress the problems created by becoming fully independent in

Headmaster Mr D. Burrell, President of the Truro School Society Dr A.K. Thould and Chairman of the School Governors, Mr J.B. Daniel inspecting the building work

status. Before this there were frequent tales of illicit trips to Truro High School boarding houses and somewhat reluctant meetings at arranged dances. Friday afternoon activities included girls from the High School coming to Truro School to have woodwork lessons and boys making the return trip for Home Economics or Textiles lessons. In 1977 a girls' team was entered in the Ten Tors competition from Truro School, though the competitors were mostly girls from the High School, who had been trained at Truro School[8].

The introduction of girls at the school met with a mixed reaction, though generally favourable. The school magazine included a droll article from the M.C.P.S. (Male Chauvinist Pig Society), written by a 'concerned converted M.C.P.', which discussed the benefits of girls at the school. They might have made a difference 'to a very small minority' and provided some distraction, but a definite improvement had been noticed in table manners and the phrase 'Morning Men!' certainly needed revising though it was sardonically seen as 'an infringement on the male chauvinistic dominance which we once had'. It was concluded that 'I think I am speaking for all of us, the more the merrier!'[9]

Among the many benefits of this change, the school, the school could at last perform a play as a whole. Reporting on the 1977 play of *The Fire Raisers* it was commented that 'there was a unity in this production that might have been helped by the fact that the girls of Truro School played the ladies' parts and not visitors (however welcome) from other schools'[10].

The main building feat was a 'do-it-yourself' project undertaken in the mid 1970s incorporating the building of a new technology block and sports hall. The project was under the direction of Dennis Keam, the technology master, and built by pupils and local craftsmen on the designs of Messrs. Marshman, Warren and Taylor, of Truro. The school, after launching a fundraising appeal in 1974, obtained financial assistance from the Job Creation

The completed technology workshop

scheme to fund the building work. The ground behind Overleigh was levelled and on 18 October 1975 the foundation stone was laid by Hawken Rose, the chairman of the County Council and an old boy of the school. Pupils carried out work on the site in the holidays, half days and the occasional private study period, and built the technical block, the walls for the sports hall and its foundation, before handing over the building work to the Job Creation scheme[11] Help was also forthcoming from old boys, parents and friends of the school. The school magazine reassured parents and pupils alike that the builders followed in the footsteps of many well-known men who had such practical experience; 'Winston Churchill found bricklaying an intriguing pastime even though the wall he built was not straight'[12].

By 1978 the new buildings had been completed. The building work marked the change in the school's status from direct grant to independent, and despite a degree of uncertainty prevalent, it was a way of 'showing confidence in the future'. A con-

Spirit of Truro, an Evans VP2 two-seater light aircraft, the first major project built in the new workshop

siderable incentive to join the state sector had been 'the near-certain promise that the new facilities in which youngsters had to work, would be provided by the local education authority', instead the school chose to be independent and construct the necessary building in their own way[13]. The opening ceremony took place with Sir Alan Dalton, deputy chairman of English China Clay as the guest speaker, who, while stressing the importance of technical education, remarked that 'education had become a political punch-bag and, along with other components of our society, suffered from a top heavy administration'. He also suggested that there was a decline in personal ambition because the state had taken over many of the responsibilities of individuals[14].

The sports hall was large enough to provide for many indoor sports including hockey, soccer, cricket and tennis. It also had a purpose built climbing wall, which at the time was only the second in the county and new changing facilities were included to accommodate the increasing number of girls who were attending the school.

The technology block included space and equipment for art, pottery, woodwork, metalwork, engineering drawing and auto engineering. 'The only graffiti on the walls of the craft centre is something the school is very proud of. It is a simple inscription to the fact that the pupils built it themselves'[15]. The building work was part of a wider celebratory appeal for the approaching centenary: a new sixth form, classrooms and an assembly hall were planned for Treliske, as well as the creation of an Assisted Places Fund to take the place of the direct grants[16].

The first project undertaken in the new technology block was the building of a full-size aeroplane. It was initially planned to build two aircraft, but it eventually became clear that only one would be completed. The construction of the Evans

The gymkhana was one of several events held by the Truro School Society to raise money for the building project

The cricket pavilion was rebuilt in the 1970s after it was destroyed by fire. It was moved to its present position in 1948, when the old field was sold off – it is now part of Truro Rugby Club

VP2 two-seater light aircraft, of American design, began in the summer term of 1978 and was intended to create interest in technology of the twentieth century. The plane was constructed from wood and ply, using the woodwork and metalwork skills of the pupils. The project involved 70 to 80 boys as an after school activity, led by Mr Keam with the help of local experts. The work was shared out between the age groups, with younger boys cutting out wooden slats and sixth formers putting the finishing touches. Two boys who worked continually on the plane were Fred Chan of Hong Kong and David Walton from Newquay.

Progress was steady, so that by January 1979 the fuselage and wings were complete, with only the fuel tank, tab trim and undercarriage still to do. When finally constructed the plane weighed 694 pounds, 'less than a Mini', had a wingspan of 27 feet and was 19 feet 3 inches in length.

The project was financed by sponsorship from several sources including BP Oil Ltd, as part of their 'Challenge to Youth' scheme, and a number of local businessmen, headed by Robert Mallet. Volkswagen Audi provided a 'generous gift' of an engine, which was converted from 1600 cc to 1834 cc to ensure there was enough power to fly. After test flights at Land's End, it was approved airworthy and registered as G-BTSC. The first public flight was planned for the visit of the Prince of Wales, who was visiting the school as part of the centenary celebrations on 20 May 1980. The flight had to be postponed due to strong winds, but Prince Charles was still able to name the plane *Spirit of Truro* during his visit[17].

The Truro School Society was reformed: arising from the crisis of the early part of the decade. Its initial priority was again to maintain close links with the Old Boys' Association, pupils, parents and staff.

The Society helped to raise money for various projects, including the building of the technology block and sports hall, through events such as concerts, gymkhanas and fashion shows.

In 1970 the school magazine was given an overhaul. It became a yearly magazine instead of having an edition each term; this was because the editorials of the last decade had frequently bemoaned the lack of willingness of people to write contributions for it. The new style magazine saw an increased amount of school artwork featured, and the 'school notes' which had been part of the magazine since the 1890s were replaced. It continued to include various amusing reports on societies, whether real

intention was 'righting historical wrongs' in the face of opposition, commended several historical figures for their service to triviality and frivolity, and as part of a field trip they planned to take a mini-bus to Room 2[19]. Meanwhile the Sixth Arts Coffee Society, 'set up to drink coffee', spent most of its time 'trying to stop an unfortunately sizeable leak in the kettle and trying to hide the stains in the wood-work'. In addition they proclaimed that 'all rumours that we are holding Cornwall's entire sugar supply in one of the lockers are completely groundless and untrue'. The Lower Sixth Whist Club was set up because of a lack of ability to play Bridge; they felt that 'acknowledgement must go to the Daily Telegraph, whose magazine was used to cover up lumps of marmalade on the card table'[20].

In 1976 poems, photographs and stories from Treliske were included in the magazine for the first time. An Old Boys' Newsletter was published in 1971 as a separate entity from the school magazine; previously there had been an old boys' section in the magazine but this had been missing for several years.

The more serious clubs and societies continued to prosper and the Debating Society was revived in 1974 after a lapse of several years. The Borlase Society stopped their excavation at Perran Sands in 1971 because it was continually flooded in bad weather and the pump used to drain it was no longer sufficient. Over the five years of digging there they had found various pieces of pottery, shell, bone, charcoal and leather. Attention was turned instead to an excavation at Longstone Down, near St Austell.

There appears to have been a resurgence of interest in conventional toys; a model railway club was formed, occasionally hijacking a classroom to layout the increasingly complicated track. This was later followed by a similar club at Treliske. By the mid 1970s there was a proliferation of war game societies, re-enacting various battles and campaigns through history with model soldiers. The widespread interest in films and cinema continued to be reflected in the school's own film festival, which had initially been set up in the late 1960s. There was an increase in the numbers involved in the school's film

or surreal, like the Salad Cream With Everything Society, as well as a report on sixth formers playing 'tag'.

The Apathy Society included a report in the 1977 school magazine, which possibly went against 'society rules to be an active member' and quipped that 'subs for 1947 are now overdue'[18]. The Catherine of Aragon Preservation Society, whose

The school under floodlights

unit and it was feared that the cinema would become more important than the written word[21].

Hockey became a more widely played sport, especially after girls became a part of the sixth form. In the early part of the decade senior day boys and boarders, as well as a prefects team played against girls' teams from Tremough and Truro High School, while in 1974 it was taken up by boys at Treliske[22]. In 1976 the cricket pavilion was burnt down, and the following year a new one, which had been designed by old boy John Crowther, was opened by the mayor of Truro, Kingsley Smith J.P. another old boy of the school[23].

The sailing club was increasingly popular despite an occasional lack of enthusiasm to get wet in capsize drills and creating a 'spectacle of boats zig-zagging all over the bay trying to capsize and then changing their minds at the last minute.

Fortunately our resident sadist was on hand in the safety boat to ensure that no-one escaped his ritual baptism'.

The Life Saving Society was having problems because of the absence of any water in the school pool[24]. but badminton was introduced despite there not being a proper court to play on until the new sports hall was built. The Under-15 seven-a-side rugby team won the county championship in 1974. After winning the first four games, the final held in St Ives was played against Newquay School:

the game itself wasn't a classic by any means, partly because of nerves and partly because of the four week gap since the earlier rounds. However, a couple of powerful runs by Pryor and a fine dummying run by Floyd all resulted in tries and we had won this competition for the third time in the last four years[25].

At Treliske there was a series of musicals produced by the school during the 1970s, including Oliver and an operatic version of Tom Sawyer. Pupils created a large papier-mâché coat of arms for the Queen's jubilee in 1977, which was displayed at the bottom of Lemon Street and the prep school also gained an addition to its collection of armour, a suit nicknamed Fred[26].

Also in this decade several long serving masters including Freddie Wilkes and Ken James retired. Ken James, a keen rugby supporter and referee, had been housemaster of Epworth and had introduced the table tennis inter-house competition and the chess team. 'Sammy' Way finally retired from teaching music due to failing eyesight; he had first come to the school in 1922[27]. Wilkes, head of modern languages and school librarian, had been actively involved in the drama society and had produced the annual school plays since 1945. Burrell recalled that the daily walks to chapel with his deputy 'were moments for his wry humour, his "common sense of proportion" attitude amidst crises and his total grasp of the life of the school'[28]. John Tonkin, who retired in 1978, succeeded Wilkes as Second Master and held the position of Acting Headmaster while Burrell was away on sabbatical in 1977. Burrell spent two terms reading 'Church History' at Bristol and Cambridge and visiting various educational establishments in England and Australia[29]. Graham Smith, formerly the chairman of the governors, retired from the governing body in 1972, aged over 90 and finally ending his family's long-standing connection to the school.

The old school uniform had been replaced in the late 1960s and since then there had been a slight relaxation of rules; hair length became longer and trousers became wider. In addition, the wearing of school caps was no longer a school rule because they were no longer believed to have a place in society; 'these date from Edwardian times when the wearing of some form of head-wear was a universal obligation'. It was also suggested (by pupils) that the sixth form not wear uniform, especially since the age of becoming an adult had been lowered[30].

Reviews of the Centenary Booklet printed in the School Magazine

As part of the celebrations of the centenary year, Mr Nigel Baker, former pupil and now on the staff of the school, was invited to produce a pictorial and written record of the school's hundred years. The result was an instructive and eminently entertaining booklet. It was reviewed both by the West Briton and the Western Morning News in the articles which appear below.

'Bed-less Start to Boarding School',
from the *Western Morning News*
Within a matter of years Truro will have had three major centenaries – of Truro itself, Truro Cathedral and Truro School.

Truro School, beginning its centenary year this winter term, has planned events which include an exhibition on Founder's Day (Jan.20.1980) which will display some dated school garments, and goes through to a final thanksgiving service in Truro Cathedral in October, 1980.

A booklet, 'Truro School Centenary', has been published and is edited by a member of staff, Mr Nigel Baker, himself an old Truro schoolboy.

In 1879 the first headmaster was appointed to a school which then only existed on paper and had no pupils or premises. Eventually premises were found using a chapel lecture hall and adjoining room as classrooms, and providing boarding accommodation at Strangways Terrace.

The account goes on to say: 'The day prior to the arrival of the boys a serious problem arose – the beds had not arrived from the manufacturers and so the 25

reminded, to set the right note, of the school's origins in the wave of educational enthusiasm that manifested itself in Victorian England, and specifically with the Bradford Methodist Conference of 1878.

But the Old Boy spirit of Bunter, Wharton and the rest soon begins to break irrepressibly through.

… We are regaled with tales of football by moonlight (v. Lelant, December 1895); of a quest for a monstrous rat inhabiting the corner of the reading room in April 1897; of the demise of Carn Brea, the school donkey, in July 1897; and of the marking of the Relief of Mafeking with a half-holiday and fireworks in July 1900.

boarders spent their first night on borrowed beds and straw mattresses.

The opening was held on Jan. 19. 1880 and the following day the first pupils assembled and the true career of the school began…

'The Day they Hunted Reading Room Rat',
from the *West Briton*

A hundred years of any school's life equals ten decades of young aspirations, exultations, hallowed moments and awful memories. The Old Boys of Truro School have rallied generously to the flag in reviving their adolescent impressions of the Alma Mater for this generous exercise in nostalgia.

Cornwall's only Headmasters' Conference school – in the words of the present headmaster, Mr Derek Burrell, 'we are one of the cheaper H.M.C. schools' – has amassed over the years a rich store of this commodity.

The Old Boys, distinguished and obscure, have done this beautifully-produced booklet proud. We are first

… More recently, since 1965, the school has weathered a quite bitter struggle between those who wanted total independence and those who wanted total alignment with the State's educational system.

The independent lobby won. The school's present headmaster, Mr Derek Burrell, writes: 'At the moment their faith appears justified, and the school's confidence has been largely sustained by the exciting building works … Personally, I enjoyed being in charge of a direct grant school, and still believe that the system was one which bridged the State provision of education (right for the majority) and the independent area (likely to persist in a free society). My own view is that boarding school education is no longer seen by so many parents as good in itself. 'Boarding need' is the great phrase of the Seventies…'

We all have our old school to remember, with varying degrees of intensity and affection. But the special warmth of this deliciously nostalgic booklet is guaranteed to get through to the most resistant 'townie' of Truro and Cornwall.

1980-1989

The Prince of Wales testing out the *Spirit of Truro*

1980 - 1989: 100 years and Beyond

By early 1980 the school centenary celebrations were fully under way. They had begun on 11 November 1979 with a firework display and at the end of term there had been a winter ball held at the Hotel Bristol in Newquay. On 20 January 1980, a service held in St Mary Clement Methodist Chapel, was followed by a celebratory boarders' tea, which included a huge birthday cake with one hundred candles[1].

Many areas of school life held activities to celebrate the occasion: the football team went on a tour to London, playing other school teams, visiting Wembley and Arsenal stadiums and managing to watch England beat Wales at rugby. The choir travelled to Coventry to give a musical recital in the cathedral and in the Methodist Coventry Central Hall.

Back at the school 750 trees, mainly pine, ash and sycamore, were planted around the grounds by first-year pupils. The old boys' reunion was held for the first time for many year in the school dining hall and was attended by more than one hundred old boys. Among them were Lowry Creed, the former headmaster, and representatives from the London branch including the chairman Roy Orford and the secretary, John Delbridge. The next day, Sunday, a service was held in the school chapel and a memorial plaque to John Tonkin was dedicated by the Reverend Tom Magson, son of the former headmaster E. H. Magson[2].

Esse Quam Videri
1. To be and not to seem to be,
A hundred years of life.
A sign of hope, a growing tree
Through all the world of strife

Chorus: A symbol bright for Cornwall's sons,
Set on a high hillside,
Esse Quam Videri

2. To be and not to seem to be,
A second hundred waits
To guide us on, to set us free
Who enter in its gates.

3. To be and not to seem to be,
How soon the years pass on.
Our work will be but memory
When days of school are gone.

4. To be and not to seem to be,
We sing our joyful song.
May more of Cornwall's sons come forth
To join our happy throng.

5. To be and not to seem to be.
Our motto good and true
Has shaped our past, for all to see.
May it shape our future too.

by S. McGrady and P. McGrady

The visit of the Prince of Wales to the school on 20 May was considered the high point of the celebrations. Following after a welcome from the headmaster and chairman of the governors, Prince Charles moved along the terrace to unveil the centenary window in the chapel, designed by a monk from Buckfast Abbey. Then after touring the school, including the new technology block, the Prince named the school aeroplane *Spirit of Truro*:

Enthusiastically the Prince, an experienced pilot himself, tested the controls and was obviously impressed by the expertise which had gone into its construction. He voiced a sentiment which was in everybody's mind when he said, 'I hope it will fly'[3].

The day after the Prince of Wales' visit the Centenary Concert was held in St Mary's and among the various musical pieces performed was the Centenary song, *Esse Quam Videri*, composed by

two pupils, Stephen and Patrick McGrady. It had first been performed the previous day when the Prince arrived at the school.

The celebrations came to a close on 5 October 1980 with a service held in the Cathedral: 'it seemed fitting that the service should be held in the Cathedral as part of the Diocesan Centenary cele-brations, since Truro School has made a contribu-tion, not only to Methodism, but to the Duchy in general and the whole Church'. The President of the Conference, who preached at the service, reflected that a vast number of changes had occurred since the school was founded and 'a ser-vice like this today in an Anglican cathedral would have been unthinkable'[4].

THE ROYAL AERO CLUB

OF THE UNITED KINGDOM

AIRCRAFT RECORD CERTIFICATE
NATIONAL BRITISH RECORD

PILOT B.P. IRISH
Truro School Flying Club
AIRCRAFT TYPE VP-2

RECORD CLASS C.1a   **DATE** 23rd July 1982

REGISTRATION G-BTSC

RECORD FLIGHT FROM MORLAIX, France.   **TO** TRURO, Cornwall.

DISTANCE 113.604	**Naut. Miles**	**SPEED** 52.77	**Knots**
130.733	**Stat. Miles**	60.73	**MPH**
210.395	**Km.**	97.73	**KPH**

Chief Timekeeper
Ray W. Kingdon

Member of the Fédération Aéronautique Internationale

Chairman
Beverley J. Snook

The school plane was the first of its kind to be built by British students. This certificate marks the return flight across the Channel, from Morlaix to Truro, which took place on 23 July 1982

The centenary was a timely occasion to remind people of the school's history. Over the previous few decades, judging from the school magazines, there had been less of a focus on earlier years in the school's history. As a result a centenary exhibition was set up depicting historical, dramatic and musical aspects. 'The present generation of boys seemed intrigued by the uniform of earlier days, especially the Eton collars, and the account books rendering details of staff salaries'[5]. In addition to the exhibition, a booklet about the history of the school was printed as a lasting record and souvenir of the centenary.

The *Spirit of Truro* took its first flight above Truro on 17 June 1981[6]. It had been planned for the flight to take place to coincide with the visit of the Prince of Wales, but it had to be postponed due to strong wind and the delay continued until the following year because of recurring problems.

During the summer of 1980 the plane was taken to a series of air shows, including the Farnborough International S.B.A.C. Flying Display and Exhibition in September. It was the first plane of its type in Britain and the first plane to be built by schoolboys, so it attracted considerable of attention; letters were received from Romania and Canada, and there was media coverage in Holland, Australia and America[7]. There had been plans to build a more complicated model, which would be entered in the 1980 Round the World Air Race, but this was put aside due to a lack of time and funds.

In July 1982 the plane, flown by Phil Irish, a former R.A.F. pilot and member of the Truro School Flying Committee, completed a flight from Truro to Morlaix in Brittany. There was no radar equipment in the plane so it flew almost at sea level and a map and compass were used to navigate. The French local newspapers appeared surprised that

The introduction of girls to the school in the late 1970s led to the provision of boarding accommodation for girls: first in Dove House which opened in 1980

such a small plane, built by schoolboys, had managed to cross the Channel; they saw it as an example of the British enthusiasm for D.I.Y. The return journey on 23 July achieved a National British Record, in 2 hours and 9 minutes, and at a speed of 52.77 knots[8]. The plane was kept at Truro Airfield for several years until it was given a more permanent home at the R.A.F. museum in Hanford.

In 1986 Derek Burrell retired as headmaster and was succeeded by Barry Hobbs. Burrell had led the school through many changes, not the least of which included surviving the troubled times associated with becoming fully independent and the introduction of girls to the sixth form. During 27 years as headmaster Burrell had 'earned a reputation as an outstanding and popular leader. Never the strictest of disciplinarians, he always saw the best of the worst pupils and his staff and his pastoral care for those around him was exceptional'[9].

Hobbs took forward many of the plans laid during Burrell's headmastership, including making the school co-educational. He had previously been headmaster of Torquay Grammar School, which had been made the first new public school for 44 years and was where Burrell had spent two terms as an evacuee from London during the Second World War[10].

In 1980 an education act established some financial support for students in independent schools with the 'assisted places scheme', which was set up to increase parental choice and participation in children's Education[11]. Another act in 1986 again sought to allow parents more involvement in the management and governorship of schools[12], though in many ways parents could already be quite involved in governing Truro School if they wanted to and had been since its foundation. By the late 1980s, G.C.S.E.s were replacing O levels as the

*The Headmaster and Governors of Truro School
have great pleasure in inviting you to attend*

A CELEBRATION
in honour of
MICHAEL ADAMS
Grandmaster and British Chess Champion
and to congratulate the
TRURO SCHOOL CHESS TEAM
on its success in The Times British Schools Chess Championship
on FRIDAY, 29th SEPTEMBER
at 7.15 p.m. for 7.30 p.m. in the School Dining Hall

R.S.V.P. *The Headmaster, Truro School
Trennick Lane, Truro*

In 1987 Michael Adams became British Chess Champion and Grandmaster while still at school

exams for 16 year olds. French and German became core subjects and there was much less Latin[13].

Locally there were quite a few changes occurring to educational facilities in Truro. Penair and Richard Lander Secondary Schools had opened in 1979, but they only catered for pupils up to the age of 16. Robin Hart, headmaster of Penair, believed that a sixth form would be beneficial for the school, but that not having one had not hindered its progress. In addition he believed that co-educational schools were 'much more natural'[14]. Plans were made for a state run sixth form college, using the girls' grammar school near the station, while in 1981 Polwhele School opened, creating competition for Treliske. The following year the Cathedral School closed and after the High School declined to merge, it later reopened as the Duchy Grammar School at Come-to-Good[15].

The main change at Truro School was that it became fully co-educational: first in Treliske in 1989 and the following year in the main school.

Dove House had been opened in 1980 to provide boarding facilities for girls in Agar Road; the boarding house was a converted vicarage. In 1987 it was proposed to make Poltisco available for girls' boarding as well.

The increase in the number of girls at the school in the sixth form, led to the creation of the first all girls hockey team in 1981. In the first year however they only played one match, against Truro High School, on a very cold and wet day: 'spirits were dampened and lower extremities – i.e. feet! were found to be missing...'[16]. A hockey team was later taken on tour to Zimbabwe, which was still suffering the effects of civil war, and the Truro School team were seen by their hosts as 'a full British representative side' playing 'test' games[17].

A variety of new sports were started including judo, basketball and archery. However during the 1980s chess gained a high profile at the school, due largely to the success of Michael Adams, who as a first year had progressed beyond county level to

Above - Computer technology was increasingly being used at Treliske and Truro School during the 1980s
Below - A game of cricket in full swing with the new cricket pavilion in the background

A view of the school from the Cathedral

A 1980s aerial view of the school, showing the building work of the late 1970s

captain the England Under 12 Team and become British Under 12 Champion. The following year he entered an International Master Qualifier match, and by 1987 he was the youngest Grandmaster[18]. Chess was not the only sport in which Truro School pupils achieved success. In 1989, beginning his sailing career, Ben Ainslie won a place in the British squad after coming fifth in the national trials in Leicestershire, and with David Lenz was selected to represent Britain in the International Optimist Championships in Japan[19]. In eventing, a new sport for the school, Anna Barrington represented Britain in the Junior European Championship[20].

In 1988, general studies on Friday afternoons, which had been in place since the 1970s, were replaced by an activities afternoon on Wednesdays. In addition to sports matches, it provided an opportunity for a wide range of extra-curricular activities, including computers and astronomy. The allotments, used by previous generations for growing crops of vegetables, most recently by the Y.F.C. in the 1970s, were sold off[21]. Public speaking was frequently participated in and the girls' teams were as successful as the boys'. In 1981 the Truro School team gained third place in the national final and Mark Prisk won a prize for best speaker and was awarded the Speaker of the House of Commons Cup[22], foreshadowing his later entry into politics.

Under the leadership of Mr Keam and Mr Crawford, the Deadstop System, a tractor safety device, was designed by pupils at the school; it received a national launch in the summer of 1987, funded by B.P, 'when it was hailed as a significant step forward in the campaign to improve farm

The school continued to produce a wide range of plays, including *The Beggars' Opera* by John Gay and an adaptation of *Tom Jones* by Henry Fielding

safety'[23]. In 1988 the Young Enterprise scheme was introduced into the sixth form, giving participants a taste of setting up and running their own business, in competition with teams from other schools[24].

School discos began in 1983 and among those who attended were '...the hopeful young Romeos, clean for the first time in the term and reeking of toothpaste.... The prospective Juliets, daubed with just a little too much woad and ... the Penairites (a neighbouring tribe whose war song begins 'Higher on the hill') who have arrived at the ceremony only to be remorselessly turned from the gates'. The magazine report on the first disco was a pastiche on a David Attenborough programme: 'slowly the great door swings open and you are battered by a tempest of noise and optical effects. The floor is, as yet, deserted, with small gregarious groups lining the gap between floor and wall. Then, as more impatient victims tentatively make their appearance, brave individuals start their own peculiar mating display...the witch-doctor gazes on, disapproving'[25]. By the end of the 1980s the leavers'

From Gilbert and Sulivan's *H.M.S. Pinafore*

ball had also become an established end of year tradition.

In 1986 Treliske celebrated 50 years since its establishment, marked by the opening of a new sports hall. In 1989 Alan Ayres retired as headmaster and was succeeded by Russell Hollins. Ayres had been resident housemaster at Treliske since 1960 (it was during that decade that the name was changed to 'headmaster'). 'He was a traditionalist. He was unhappy about the disappearance of Saturday morning school, and some of the great traditions he established included a very 'trad' speech day (hats and all), the musicals on those occasions, and the Sunday morning services'.

Hollins, who had previously been headmaster of the Royal Wolverhampton Junior School, was by comparison more modern in approach and endorsed the idea of girls attending Treliske, because he declared '…an all-male environment to be an unrealistic reflection on society – and that it is important to acknowledge the academic prowess of the girls!'[26]

The school library moved to its present position in the mid 1980s, taking the place of the War Memorial Library, which is now the staff room, and reopening as the Rule Memorial Library in 1986. Similarly the old gym above the chapel was converted into a common room for the lower sixth form[27]. Burrell's departing wish, made in his final address to the school, was for a purpose-built drama facility at the school. The school's interest in theatre was again exemplified when the Royal Shakespeare Company staged performances of *The Beaux' Stratagem* and *A Midsummer Night's Dream* in the sports hall and later returned with *Romeo and Juliet*[28] thus inspiring the school's own productions. Former pupil Benjamin Luxon chaired a meeting on 26 October 1989 launching the Hall for Cornwall campaign, to convert the old town hall into a theatre[29].

Truro School was set to expand further, both in physical size and in numbers. This would begin with the admittance of girls from the age of eleven for the first time in September 1990.

Barry Hobbs, the seventh headmaster

B.Hobbs (1986 – 1992)

Barry Hobbs was at Truro School for six years and during that relatively brief time the school changed a great deal under his headmastership. Among the changes a new library was installed in the former Tower dormitory, the sick bay was modernised, a new biology laboratory was built and the old gym was converted into a common room for the lower sixth. In addition the teaching departments were reorganised to make them more compact and the pre-prep school at Treliske was opened. The main feature of his tenure, however, must be the introduction of co-education throughout the school.

Co-education brought inevitable changes but connections to the past and the school's traditions remained, so that the radical change was tempered somewhat. There were also changes made to the curriculum, with the introduction of G.C.S.E.s, not only in the standard subjects but also new subjects such as Media Studies and Physical Education. Hobbs was also a keen supporter of the school's Christian Union[1].

Barry Hobbs went to university in London before taking up his first teaching post in Guilford. After this he became deputy head of a school in Southend. He came to Truro School from Torquay Grammar School where he had been headmaster for four and a half years. At that time Torquay was the first new public school for 44 years.

In an interview for the school magazine he cited his role of headmaster at Truro School 'as the creator of a synthesis between the old and the new'. He believed that he had come 'to a very special school', whose roots were firmly embedded in tradition, but stressed that Truro School should not be allowed to stand aside from the march of progress; 'we must not become a museum at any cost'[2], a feeling that was held by many other long-established schools[3]. Changes to the school would be made but every effort was made to maintain the high standards.

In another interview for the school magazine, when asked what alternative career he might have chosen, Hobbs responded:

If I couldn't be a teacher I'd like the job of Sir Humphrey Appleby because 'Yes Minister' is my favourite television programme (It was also Mrs Thatcher's!!) and I would like to play that role. I wouldn't mind being a museum curator but not an archivist – I would want a job that involved working with people[4].

In the Lent term of 1992 Hobbs announced that he would not be able to continue as headmaster the following September due to ill health. As a result the deputy head, Brian Jackson, acted as head, until a permanent successor, Guy Dodd, was able to take up the position the following year.

Guy Dodd, the eighth headmaster

G. Dodd (1993 – 2001)

Guy Dodd was known for his 'phenomenal memory for names'[1]. He retired from Truro School at the end of the summer term 2001, after nine years at the school. He had come to Truro after holding the post of headmaster at Lord Wandsworth College in Hampshire for ten years. He was educated at Cheltenham College and went on to read history and geography at Emmanuel College, Cambridge. His first teaching post was in King's College in Auckland, New Zealand but he later returned to his old school in Cheltenham as history teacher and housemaster[2].

When he came to Truro in September 1993 the school was going through uncertain times once again: government assisted places were about to be phased out, pupil numbers were declining and co-education was making slow progress in the school, not helped by strong competition from the newly opened sixth form college in Truro. Any

difficulties that the school was going through were also highlighted, and possibly intensified, by the introduction of league tables. Consequently 'not for the first time in its history, the school was at a cross-roads'. To overcome the problems several plans were set in motion. It was decided that it was necessary to reduce the school's debt to zero. In addition, fundraising, in the form of an endowment appeal, was established to provide the school's own assisted places, 'so that the doors of the school could remain as wide as possible following the end of Government Assisted Places Scheme'[3].

As a result of the alterations the finances became much healthier, which in turn led to the possibility of new classrooms being provided at both Treliske and the main school. The music facilities were moved to a reorganised Epworth from 'a hut at the bottom of the drive'. The swimming pool was properly housed and roofed, transforming it from an open-air pool into one for all year round use; it was opened in 1996 by Olympic swimmer Nick Gillingham. The lack of drama facilities continued, as did the lack of car parking space, but a new hard surface play area was added to the inside of the athletics track, the dining hall was refurbished, the boarding accommodation was reorganised and a school-wide computer network was installed.

'Then the culmination of his nine years – the Burrell Theatre and new classroom block', were built, finally putting an end to the lack of performing arts facilities[4].

Guy Dodd, as headmaster, was at the forefront of these changes. During his time in office there was continued and increased achievement in exams, as well as in various sports. He also introduced the twice-weekly lunches with sixth formers.

Outside of the school, Dodd was a member of the Admiralty Interview Board, a governor of three preparatory schools, a member of the committee of the Clergy Orphan Corporation, the Professional Development Committee of the Headmasters' Conference and the Awarding Panel of Joint Education Trust[5]. After leaving Truro School he spent a 'gap year' travelling to Nicaragua, Australia and New Zealand with his wife, Helen, before coming back to Cornwall.

1990-1999

School Governors in May 1995 - Standing (left to right): Barry Grime, District Judge Christopher Tromans, Patricia Kent, Cyril Harding, Elizabeth Wilton, Rev Dr Stephen Dawes, John Keast, Rev Gerald Burt, Jo Toms
Sitting: Robert Cowie, Geoffrey Rumbles, Elizabeth-Ann Malden, David Jewell (Vice-Chairman) , John Heath (Chairman), George Owens, Derek Robson, Christine Roberts

1990 – 1999:
Shaking off the Bonds of Tradition

The beginning of the 1990s was marked by the school becoming fully co-educational, accepting girls from the first year upward, not just in the sixth form, as before. The girls, though initially outnumbered by the boys, 'quickly merged into the school, and [became] part of the 'scenery' without, it seems, too many 'teething' problems'. The headmaster proclaimed that 'we have shaken off the bonds of our tradition', while a newspaper quipped 'forget Tom Brown's schooldays, Truro School has just gone partially co-educational'[1].

The majority of the schools in the Headmasters' Conference admitted girls by this point, who made up 25,535 out of 153,179 pupils, though the schools' hierarchy remained predominantly male. By 1990 at Truro School 16 out of 67 full time teachers were female and there were five women among the 21 governors[2]. The men continued to hold the senior positions however, and the headmaster, Hobbs, in an article for the school magazine, commented that

in very few schools are women in senior positions. It takes time – it is a matter of evolution rather than revolution. The difficulty is getting women to apply – one must also be careful of 'positive bias', you have to choose the best candidate for the job in the interest of both staff and pupils and not enough women are coming forward.

Despite there being more women teachers than men nationally, the majority taught predominantly in junior schools. In 1991 the school was gradually

Rising ballet stars – a change from the traditional boys' sports and activities that have dominated attention in the past

brought by the admittance of girls included the calling of pupils by their first names instead of by their surnames. Similar to their predecessors in the 1970s, in some circles it was felt that boys were disciplined more strictly, while the girls were treated more favourably because teachers felt the 'need to restrain themselves in the presence of females'. Calls for fair treatment to both boys and girls continued because it was believed that 'only when both boys and girls are treated equally and fairly will Truro School be truly co-educational'[4].

In September 1994 a new school kilt was introduced for girls in the first to the fifth forms, changing from the various forms of grey skirt that had been the norm. It meant that they now had their own specific uniform rather than a leftover from the boys' uniform. The tartan was made up of the school colours of blue, white and brown. The issue of girls wearing trousers was also raised; the sixth form questionnaire in the school magazine noted that

all males were in favour of the kilt and/or the compulsory wearing of short skirts (Yawn) and felt that if trousers were to be worn by females then they in turn should be afforded the privilege of wearing a kilt; perhaps with a sporran?? The females in our midst were anti kilts and felt there would be too much opposition from the powers that be to trousers[5].

The change to the status quo of pupils was not easy initially, meeting a little resistance in both the prep and senior schools. Sixteen girls entered the prep school in September 1989, bringing the total number of pupils at Treliske up to 157. Early in that term there was a 'startling lack of integration' between boys and girls:

Both sets were quick to recognise this, with the boys loudly complaining that the girls stay in groups ... The boys referred to the girls as, horrible things from outer space! Although perhaps is just a resentment of the modicum of civilisation and sophistication which arrived with them. Despite this professed aversion, the girls were quick to tell us of the manner in which they were eagerly pursued on first arrival!

increasing the number of women teachers employed, with Mrs Weeks as deputy head of the sixth form and Miss Leathes, the new head of Wickett house. There were also three form tutors for the new mixed forms in the 3rd year 'so there was no lack of approachable female staff'[3].

Although a small number of girls had been admitted to the sixth form since the 1970s, the new intake highlighted the limitations of school facilities, subjects and extra-curricular activities. This was to be expected to some degree, until there had been enough time for the girls' presence at the school to become more established. Changes

Chess continues to thrive at the school

Girls joined in sports like hockey and football and 'new' subjects such as C.D.T, although they had some separate lessons, such as dancing. There was a little resentment from the boys that the girls appeared more successful and did not get detentions. However by the end of the first term grudges and divisions died away, and everyone appeared to have 'risen to this challenge, both pupils and teachers alike'. It was quickly apparent that 'despite the recent introduction of girls, there now seemed few traces of their ever having been absent at Treliske'[6]. In September 1990, several of the first intake of younger girls to the senior school found it a little daunting initially.

The thought of being one out of twenty-five girls was a sufficiently daunting prospect, but the thought of being in a form of boys, some of whom had never ever been to school with a girl in their lives was awful.

On the first morning, all the new people were con-gregated in the chapel... were then told to go to their form rooms. We left our friends as they went off to their respective form rooms until there was only eight of us left cowering behind the door of room forty-eight debating as

Rugby on the first team pitch, now the Astroturf
all-weather surface

to who would enter the room first. When we entered, we
were greeted by mixed reactions but it looked as though
the boys had been briefed how to treat us while we were
in the chapel.

... Now that we have or think we have been accepted, life isn't quite so difficult as it was at first. The boys
can still be male chauvinists but we have learned that
retaliating is not always the answer and it is best to
ignore them. All in all, I think that the bringing of
co-education into third year was, and has turned out to
be, a good idea[7].

In 1990, E.J. Taylor retired from his position as
second master. This provided an opportunity to
restructure the senior management team so that the
second master and senior master posts were
replaced by two deputy head positions, filled by
Brian Jackson and Simon Price. One oversaw the
day-to-day discipline and pastoral matters of the
school, general school administration, and under-

took the role of director of studies, while the other
oversaw boarding, extra curricular activities, school
publications and special events. Taylor took up the
position of registrar to deal with the increasing
number of admission applications[8]. It was
becoming evident that the headmaster and his
deputies had increasingly administrative roles and it
was harder to maintain a balance with teaching.
Hobbs felt that it 'wouldn't be fair on the pupils to
be a head and a teacher because one would always
turn up late for lessons'; the position being more
like that of a businessman than a teacher. He did
however manage to take the Oxbridge maths
classes because of their flexible times[9].

In 1992, Hobbs' sudden departure from the
school due to illness meant that Brian Jackson, the
senior deputy head, took on the role of acting headmaster because it was halfway through the school
year. By April 1993 a new headmaster had been
appointed to start the following September: Guy
Dodd moved to Truro from his position as
headmaster of Lord Wandsworth College in
Hampshire. Brian Jackson retired from teaching in
July 1994, after 37 years at Truro School. The
school magazine recorded his achievements and
concluded that *he was, by his own admission, a 'boffin',
a backroom boy rather than a front man. Nothing then
had prepared him (mentally, at least) for the interreg-
num ... and his abrupt elevation to a position with oner-
ous responsibility, limited power and temporary status.
For some it would have been the short straw; for B.J. it
was both a challenge and a duty he could not shirk.*
He brought to the role stability and reassurance at a
difficult time; 'his willingness to listen and to
consult and his dogged unflappable temperament
were priceless assets'[10].

The school was affected by changes within
Truro during the 1990s. By 1993 a new tertiary college had opened in Gloweth - Truro College[11], and
though providing much needed sixth form
education for state schools, it also provided an
attractive alternative for pupils who might have
attended Truro School. Consequently there was a
slight lull in the number of applications for the sixth
form. Unlike previous occasions, the school was
able to benefit to a certain degree from the closure

of Tremough School in Penryn in the late 1990s, by offering an alternative option to the girls of Tremough.

In 1991 Truro was twinned with Boppard in Germany[12], which brought with it a renewed interest in foreign exchange and school trips to both France and Germany. In 1994 a party visited Nuremburg, which was thought

something of a marvel. What Germany has succeeded in restoring, considering that damage to the city by 1945 was 85%, is most impressive. You can walk through sections of the Altstadt and, ignoring the odd car or streetlight, might well believe yourself back in the time of the Mastersingers. A full return to the pre-war glories is now out of the question, but much has been made of what little remained.

Among the various visits to historical and cultural sites, there were also more frivolous highlights. 'Warwick's tussle with the bar-stool in the Altstadt will… linger, as will the look of mild terror on George's face as he began to take seriously the prospect of defeat at Scrabble – at the hands of a girl!'[13].

German exchange trips were organised with the Kaiser Wilhelm Gymnasium (grammar school) in Hanover, with German students visiting Truro in October and the return visit made in February. In addition a number of German sixth formers stayed at the school for one, two or three terms, joining the lower sixth to improve their English and taste life at an English boarding school, which most found 'enjoyably different from the cosmopolitan cities of the north German plain'[14].

Trips to France were equally as successful as those to Germany and featured several trips to Paris. A group of sixth formers visited Paris in October 1994 and included a number of French lectures among their activities, which had a few drawbacks because of language problems. 'These included talks and shows by R.A.T. (Regie Autonomne des Transports Parisiens) and U.N.E.S.C.O. (United Nations Educational, Scientific and Cultural Organisation). These talks would probably have been more interesting and informative had we

understood more of them, especially Jaroslav whose failure to understand, let alone speak any French, left him totally bewildered as to what was going on'. Talks were also given at the Palais de Justice which appeared to be beyond the comprehension of most. The same trip included a stay in Rouen, where the last lecture on the fission of uranium was 'surprisingly the most interesting because we were given a tour and talk at the Paluel Nuclear Power Station – in English and therefore the only one that was understood in its entirety'[15]. The French exchange was organised with pupils from the College St Joseph in Landerneau, in Brittany. In addition, by 1996 an exchange trip was established with Jakintska Ikastola School in Ordizia, a village in the Basque region of Spain, giving a valuable insight into Spanish life for members of the upper sixth studying Spanish[16].

School trips to France and Germany laid the foundation for trips further afield. A school party had visited Russia in 1989, and in 1991 another trip was made, visiting Moscow and Leningrad. The trip included a visit to a Moscow school and coping with the black market, because the inflation rate had reached 'a staggering forty-eight roubles to the £'. Nigel Baker recorded for the school magazine that

it was both a holiday and an experience. Some learned a lot, that Russian champagne and Russian chocolate really don't mix. That yes, sir was actually going to confiscate all the vodka bought on the black market, that one really can eat cucumber at every meal and that even tongue can be tasty and that the … guide can be attractive, fun and have an excellent repertoire of anti-communist jokes, not all of them especially clean[17].

In the late 1990s members of the school undertook a three-year project to raise money for the White Cross Mission, to purchase a house in Romania for orphan children and their foster parents. Earlier, in 1991, a small party had visited the village of Remeti in Western Romania and saw the condition of the orphanage for themselves[18]. By 1998 enough money had been raised to buy a house, Casa Anoushka, in Remeti, and a group from Truro School went out to meet the new family, made up of

Surfing became an increasingly popular sport at the school during the 1990s. Mark Baker

seven children and their foster mother and father. While in Romania the group also visited other orphanages, or spitals, and saw at first hand the changes that the money raised had brought to the lives of the seven children they had helped[19].

Geography field trips were becoming more exotic; in 1998 a sixth form group travelled around Iceland, visiting hot springs, extinct volcanoes and waterfalls[20]. Trips abroad were also made for sport; rugby tours were arranged to South Africa and Canada, a hockey team went to a snow covered Belgium and skiing trips were made to the Alps. Similarly several old boys were playing sports in various parts of the world: Jack Williams (1950-57) played rugby for Jamaica, Martin Fowler (1958 – 65) played cricket for the Philippines, Robert Jenkin (1949-56) a dentist in the Arabian Gulf played rugby for the Seychelles[21].

In addition to the usual sports at the school, net-ball became a permanent fixture after girls joined the school in 1990 and water polo was restarted after a break of ten years. Among the extra curricu-lar activities were show jumping and ballet. It was noticeable that during the 1990s there was an increased number of individual achievements in sport in addition to team successes. The mixed success of the cricket team was outdone by individual successes; several players played for the county side, including Tom Sharp, Charlie Shreck, and the first girl in the team, Laura Harper, 'a lethal off-break bowler', who went on to gain a place in the England side in 2000. Similarly in rugby there was an increasing number of boys playing for the county or having trials for the South West England XV. A new competition was introduced in memory of an old boy, John Kendall-Carpenter, with the school play-ing against Wellington College, where he had been headmaster, for the Kendall-Carpenter Cup. Truro won the first match 27 – 19[22].

The school golf team, of Mark Bracey, Steve Richardson, Marc Bicknell and Philip Rowe, became the national winners in 1993, after reaching the finals of the H.M.C. National Foursomes Tournament in four successive years. Philip Rowe

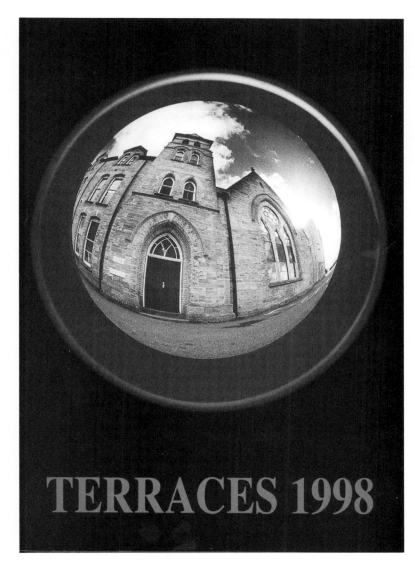

TERRACES 1998

the tournament nine times. With increased experience and practice, new skilled players emerged; Roland Cole and Andrew Greet were selected to play chess for the Young England team and the school team became the Cornish schools' champions. In 1993 Cole was in the under 21 England team playing against Denmark, and the same year the school finally won The Times British Schools Championship. 'The win at last put Truro on top in the country and reconfirmed the school's chess-playing reputation, which reached a peak when Michael Adams, who left four years ago, was made a Chess Grandmaster. Michael is now the highest-rated player after Nigel Short, who is about to bid for the world title'[23].

The 'gales, rain and weather notwithstanding ... in a bitterly-fought challenge that was concluded with strawberries and cream on the front terrace', croquet enjoyed a brief spell of popularity, bringing with it echoes of a past era at the school. Sixty four participants took part in the sixth form croquet challenge in 1990, and after a 'bitterly fought' contest the championship went to Eric Wedlake and James Pritchard[24].

became one of the youngest golfers ever to be selected by the English Golf Union for professional training at the age of 13. Success also continued on the water, with Ben Ainslie, David Lenz, Matthew Slater, Verity Slater, Nicola Barnes and Helen Morgan sailing in various classes at regional, national and international level; Adam Hale and Tom Allen in windsurfing and Matthew Barlow in surfing.

In 1990 the school chess team again won through to the finals of the British Schools Chess Championships, getting to the grand final but being beaten in the end by St Paul's, previous winners of

George Rowell and Harry Oram came third in the National Scrabble Championships held in London in November 1993. Interest in the game continued when in 1996, a school team entered the National Clubs' Championship and did very well, but lost to the eventual winners, the 'Devon Dimwits'. By the following year David Trethewey and Harry Oram became under-16 national Scrabble champions[25].

Pupils from the Pre-Prep School at Treliske, which opened in the early 1990s

In 1993 the school magazine was given a dramatic face-lift. Over the previous few years there had been less enthusiasm for producing the magazine and articles were predominantly made up of questionnaires, agony aunt pages and astrology. There had also been some criticism that the centenary of the magazine had passed by unnoticed in 1991. The new magazine continued to raise students' questions and other issues but was enlarged in size and given a more modern layout, as well as including more reports of school activities from the year. In some ways the magazine had reverted back to an earlier form, with a teacher as the editor which gave it a slightly more serious approach. Vivienne Neale was the first editor of the new style magazine, and commented that at first the 'editorial committee found themselves, to a certain extent, redundant due to technology. Who says that schools do not reflect the changing world around them?' If pupils found themselves a little redundant from the magazine production, this was eventually altered by the production of several other publications, including *Apparatus Criticus*, *The U-Bend* produced by the third year, and *Rigor Mortis* by sixth form history students. During the early 1990s there were also calls for a means of having opinions and views on school issues heard within the school on a more regular basis, and it was frequently suggested that a school council be formed[26].

The decade saw increased emphasis on business enterprise and careers. 1990 was the first time for a while that a careers convention had been put on at the school and 'represented a considerable step forward in the School's careers provision and ... [gave] a blueprint for the future'[27]. An increasing number of fifth formers undertook work experience in various businesses all over the country, in all sectors of employment. Popular choices included medicine, law and journalism, while others included air maintenance at R.N.A.S. Culdrose, working in an art gallery or museum, or working with ground staff at a county cricket club. Several older pupils participated in the Young Enterprise Scheme, creating their own businesses and attempting to make a profit by selling a variety of items, culminating in a trade fair and competing with other Cornish teams for success in marketing and other areas of business management. There were also several individuals who carried out feats of design; Keran Royale designed a kneeling chair to help prevent back pain, while Alastair Fletcher designed a yacht for his A-level design project[28].

From *The Good Woman of Setzuan,*
by Bertold Brecht, performed in 1996

By September 1993 Malvern Lodge had been renovated for use as a girls' boarding house, with extensive redesigning inside to provide accommodation for 36 girls. Pentreve and Malvern were then run as a single house under the supervision of Mrs Pam Harris and at the same time Trennick boarding house was being updated, to make the accommodation less antiquated. Not long after, Petherton House, another girls boarding house, was closed and the girls accommodated at the school instead. The junior boys' house, Trewinnard Court was closed in 1995 in response to the shrinking numbers of boarders, and to bring all boarding accommodation on to the school site, the boys were housed in an extended Poltisco House[29].

An appeal had been launched in 1990 to develop the facilities of the school further:

Already, in anticipation of the 1990s and of the transformations which co-educational status will bring, the school has invested heavily in updated academic, sporting and domestic facilities ... Now at the threshold of this decade, we wish to carry out vital improvements to our cultural amenities, and so complete the current series of improvements across the spectrum of school activities[30].

The redevelopment of the school in the previous decade included the refurbishment of the library, the enlargement of the sixth form centre, new science laboratories, and the opening of a new boarding house, Trewinnard. In addition a new athletics track, all-weather hockey pitch and tennis court were installed and the swimming pool was refurbished. The next stage was a new gymnasium with changing facilities which Sebastian Coe, Member of Parliament and former Olympic medallist, opened in 1991. Its adjustable climbing wall was the design of Justin Laupetre who had been a pupil at the school between 1982 and 1989. Plans also included a performing arts centre. The growing number of pupils increased the demand for improved and enlarged facilities for music and drama because there was only 'a limited number of things one can perform in the Chapel'[31]. By the late 1990s the tuck shop had closed and was replaced by three snack machines which 'automatically switch off during lesson time!'[32].

The pre-prep school at Treliske was officially opened by Sir John Banham, Director General of the Confederation of British Industry, in June 1992. It was named after Bert Willday, who had taught at Truro School from 1921 to 1960 and had died the previous year. It was built as a self-contained unit

The X-Files: the Staff Panto 1996 featuring Messrs. Baines, Blake and Cornish

but with easy access to Treliske's facilities; 'it incorporates four separate form bases, each within its own activity area. These are positioned around a central hall. Other features of the school are the resources centre and a large tarmac playground'[33]. The head of the new pre-prep was Mrs Jane Grassby, and the new building marked the widely increased age range of children at the school as a whole, from three to eighteen, especially when compared to a hundred years previously when the youngest pupil was eight years old and the average leaving age of was fourteen.

The need for new drama facilities was again reinforced with the return of the Royal Shakespeare Company in October 1992 and 1993; performing *Richard III* and *Julius Caesar* in the sports hall[34]. There was a wider interest in drama and the performing arts at the school with the introduction of speech and drama lessons, working towards L.A.M.D.A. awards, and the school plays have involved an increasing number of people, as well as becoming more ambitious. Epworth had been refurbished to provide better facilities for music but a large rehearsal and performing space was still needed. The theatre was not finally completed until 2002.

Review of the Staff Pantomime, *The X-Files,* from the school magazine

'Time to Close *The X-Files*'

The school waited with baited breath, rumours circulated wildly as the resurrection of the staff pantomime loomed. I hear the convention used to be quite a professional affair. In 1990 this idea was scotched when I took over and directed Cinderella. In fact it was alluded to by the Mayor, Peter Lang, in his inaugural speech. He shocked everyone by saying that the last time he appeared on stage in the chapel he was dressed as a gorilla suit and was hanging off the door eating a banana. Thus the stage was set for the latest offering. Andrew Mulligan scaled the heights and produced *The X-Files*.

The audience was quite bemused as the theme music began and mysterious images appeared on the back wall. Bianca Toy felt: 'The opening was very successful and created a sense of anticipation in the audience. We couldn't wait to discover who the teachers were under their disguises'. Jonathan Green thought 'the acting was brilliant but the mistakes made it even funnier'.

The audience was certainly shocked at the behaviour of the Senior Mistress and we wondered how many 'Fridays' she had to endure for the 'fags in the chapel' routine. In fact Mrs Biggs and Mrs Weeks brought the house down with their 'have strepsil' gag. An anonymous reviewer had this to say about Mrs Harris and Mr Mulligan: 'Scully and Mulder better watch out as Harris and Mulligan are hot on your heels'.

The staff in the audience waited nervously at the back praying they wouldn't be picked on. Unfortunately Mr Tall had fallen for the 'We need someone in the front row to look after the kiddies' line and sure enough he ended up with a first class custard pie and soda siphon shower much to the audience's delight. The ugly sisters and fairy god mother were the picture of elegance and no doubt await their call from Ms Westwood for her next London Fashion Week outing.

Yet the star of the show had to be Mr Price. Certainly his credibility ratings shot off the clapometer. There were many comments about his performance including: 'I'll never be able to take Wednesday afternoon activities in quite the same way'. 'Mr Price, it's time to go blonde!'

Certainly pupils felt they would never be able to take particular members of staff seriously again: Mr Nicholas and his exploding appendages or Mr Dodd's sympathetic approach to Smeg. They were very pleased to see staff willing and able to make fools of themselves...

Overall the pupils voted the panto a huge success and were impressed that the idea was based on something all the school could relate to. One of the fifth form said: 'I think the play achieved everything it set out to do, everyone loved it and no one kept a straight face. The only criticism is that it should have been longer'.

Now, what about South West Enders next year of Carry on Inspectors or Great Wall Displays of China, Jurassic Park (!) or Prisoner Smith Block G?...

V.K.N.

2000 - 2004

Postscript: 2000 – 2004

In the early part of the 'Noughties', Truro School has continued to be both busy and successful in all aspects of school life.

Interest in the school's history has been revived with the approach of the 125th anniversary since its foundation; an increase in the memories and historical insights being included in school publications, a reorganisation and re-evaluation of the school archives. Consequently the school has made sure of its place in the present, while looking forward to the future and not forgetting its past.

By the late 1990s the Old Boys' Association had been renamed the Truro School Association because by this time there was an increasing number of old girls eligible to join. Change continued in 2000 when it was decided that the name of the association should reflect its purpose more; consequently it was renamed the Truro School Former Pupils' Association.

The endowment appeal set up in 2000 to provide assisted places and scholarships at the school included a number of former pupils among the contributors. Also in 2000 a reunion was organised with Kent College, marking the 60th anniversary since it had been evacuated to Truro in 1940. On the first weekend of July, 14 of the former evacuees and 17 of their Truro contemporaries met at the school. Much of the time was spent revisiting sites in Truro where the Kent College had spent the war years; 'one of the current owners was surprised to find a group of senior citizens knocking at her back door. As pupils they were used to using the back door of the house!' This was followed by an excursion down the river to Falmouth and an evening banquet in the school dining hall, where 'nostalgic conversations continued long into the night'[1].

Since the 1960s and 1970s there had been calls to create a new register of former pupils and staff, to allow people to keep in touch more easily with their peers. The first, a printed version, had been produced in 1954, with yearly reprints until 1959. In 1990 it was again planned to draw up a new register, but it was not until the late 1990s with the widespread use of the Internet that it became more feasible and easier to accomplish. By 2003 the school's *Web Alumnus* site was running, allowing former pupils to keep informed of school news and events, as well as promoting networking amongst members and encouraging them to keep their own information current and relevant.

The turn of the century was marked at Treliske with the erection of new classrooms, appropriately named the Millennium Building, which included new art and design facilities[2].

The Burrell Theatre was opened in 2002 by Sir Tim Rice, who spoke to staff, pupils and guests before touring the new building, which includes a 250-seat theatre and six classrooms. He thought it quite apt that he should be associated with a school theatre project after his early success of *Joseph and the Amazing Technicolor Dream Coat*, which was especially written for a school production.

The new theatre won an award in the Highly Commended Category from the Cornish Buildings Group, 'whose representatives have spoken of the "wow factor" in its design and architecture'[3]. The first public performances in the new theatre included a jazz concert the previous December and a choral and orchestral concert that February: both occasions showed the 'wonderful acoustics for … the debut of the Music Department at this venue … [which] encouraged the young players to give of their best in an evening of high achievement'[4].

On 19 October 2004 the Wilkes Building for modern languages was opened. It was named after Cyril 'Freddie' Wilkes, former head of modern languages and deputy head, and it was opened by a former pupil of Wilkes', Graham Russell, secretary of the Methodist Schools Group.

Over the last few years there has been some change at the top in both Truro School and Treliske. At the end of the 2001 summer term, Guy Dodd retired as headmaster of Truro School and Paul Smith was appointed his successor. Having been educated at a state grammar school in Buckinghamshire, where he played rugby, cricket and hockey for the school and county, Paul Smith studied geography at Cambridge. In his final year at school he had a rugby trial for the England

The Millennium Building at Treliske opened in 2000

Schoolboys and his enthusiasm for sport continued while at university, playing rugby and cricket, rowing and gaining a Blue under the captaincy of Gerald Davies. After a brief spell in a national bank, he returned to education to take up teaching, initially as a geography teacher at St John's School, Leatherhead, where he became master in charge of rugby, head of geography, and a boarding housemaster. Then he moved with his family to Worcester, taking up an appointment as Second Master of the Royal Grammar School. After eight years, he moved to Shropshire to become headmaster of Oswestry School, where he stayed for six years before coming to Truro[5]. During his first year at the school Paul Smith paid tribute to his predecessor and laid plans for the future:

Guy Dodd has left the school in very good heart as the examination successes have revealed but, more than that, morale is high and the range and quality of extra-curricular activity reflects a vibrant and successful school. Equally importantly, the product of this special education is young men and women who are confident without being arrogant and intelligent but independent thinkers who care for their fellow men and the world they live in.

We are anxious to preserve accessibility of this most unique education opportunity and the Endowment Fund

…enables us to build upon the traditions of the school and maintain the breadth of intake[6].

He also stressed that 'in an era where 'education, education, education' is dominated by examination, examination, examination …a real education should 'enlarge, enlighten and enliven'[7]. the lives of students and staff alike.

In the summer of 2003 headmaster Russell Hollins left Treliske to take up a new post as headmaster of Chapter House School, the preparatory department of Queen Ethelberga's College in Yorkshire. Before his successor arrived in December, Jane Grassby took on the role of acting-head. Matthew Lovatt's arrival at Treliske, with his family, was met with a 'warm welcome' from Mother Nature and no heating, telephones or fire alarms because on Boxing Day

a freak bolt of lightening struck a tree in the grounds…The tree was saved from decimation by an old cable left in the ground from when the swimming pool was built. The charge of millions of volts travelled almost instantaneously from one end to the other, which lay buried in the floor of the changing rooms. On arrival it blew super-heated concrete out into the walls, ceiling and doors, leaving a crater the size of a fist. Maybe it was just as well it was the holidays[8].

Reunion of former pupils from Truro School and Kent College in 2000, marking the 60th anniversary of Kent College's evacuation to Truro in 1940. Front row (left to right): R. Andrew (T.S.1940-1), T. Vokes (T.S.1939-45), G. Austin (K.C.1937-43), P. Cox (K.C. Former Pupils' Chairman), G. Stickells (K.C.1943-56), J. Dixon (K.C. 1939-44) Second row: A. Carveth (T.S.1939-48), G. Bailey (K.C.1940-44), A. Charlesworth (T.S. 1940-47), I. Murdoch (T.S.1942-48), J. Bunney (T.S.1936-43), I. Goodhand (T.S. 1935-46), N. Bliss (K.C.1941-51) Third row: A. Brown (T.S.1937-43), I Edwards (K.C.1943-47), P. Pelmear (T.S.1936-45), R. Tchertoff (T.S.1940-45), P. Jeffery (K.C.1940-46), E. Thomas (T.S.1940-44), J. Clymo (T.S.1939-46), G. Heyworth (T.S.1945-50), John Gibson (K.C.1944-52) Back row: A. Castle (K.C.1945-50), E. Halse (K.C. Headmaster), E. Dagless (K.C.1945-51), R. Handscomb (K.C.1940-45), S. Floyd (T.S. Former Pupils' Vice-Chairman), D. Mitchell (K.C.1941-46), D. Bear (K.C.1942-51), D. Castling (T.S. Former Pupils' Chairman), G. Dodd (T.S. Headmaster), D. Tregenza (T.S.1940-43), D. Norris (T.S.1936-42), J. Foster (K.C.1939-44), D. Rowe (T.S.1942-46)

The official opening of the Wilkes Building, a new modern languages department, in October 2004, by Graham Russell, Secretary of the Methodist Schools' Group and former pupil of the school who was taught by Freddie Wilkes. To his immediate left is the Chairman of Truro School Governors, John Baxter, and to his right is Headmaster Paul Smith. Also pictured are the modern language teachers, former pupils, governors and former staff.

Truro School Lodge No. 5630
From Thread of Gold by D. Williams

'A meeting of Past Masters of lodges who were old boys of Truro School was held on 27 October 1935. The object was to 'petition Grand Lodge to form a craft lodge in connection with the school'. This was unanimously agreed and membership was restricted to old boys, past and present masters of the school and governors, with the cost kept as low as possible. The consecration took place in the school hall on 24 September 1936, performed by the Provincial Grand Master R.W. Bro. Lord St Levan, assisted by his officers... Whilst at Truro School the lodge normally met in the school hall but there were other venues: during 1938 some meetings were held in the new science block.... During the earlier years of the war when the number present was small and there was a blackout of the school hall some meetings were held in the prefects' room, the boys' common room and the art room...'

The Truro School Freemason Lodge was consecrated on 24 September 1936. Dr Magson was installed as the first Worshipful Master. Above are present day members

Past Masters of Truro School Lodge (No. 5630)	
1936	E.H. Magson
1937	W.C. Smith
1938	J.W. Hunkin
1939	N. Stringer
1940	W.F. Jewell
1941	W.R. Lobb
1942	E.P. Adams
1943	A.J. Roberts
1944	W.C. Argall
1945	C.R. Harding
1946	F.W. Truscott
1947	T. Stratton
1948	C.F. Wilkes
1949	G.B. Rundle
1950	A.H.R. Lilley
1951	W.H. Hall
1952	J.R. Slater
1953	G.E.H. Harding
1956	G.J. Hendra
1961	E.S. Vincent
1969	A.H. Freeman
1970	R.J. Julyan
1971	W.H.L. Pearce
1972	J.O. Roberts
1973	T.R.E. Trenerry
1974	R. Trenerry
1975	W.H.E.A. Thomas
1976	S.G. Heyworth
1977	B.C. Teague
1978	T. Greenslade
1979/80	P.J.M. Roberts
1983	A.R.G. Vigus
1988	E.F.J. Purkis
1989	R.R. Barnicoat
1990	W.G. Roberts
1992	B.J. Smith
1993	D.J. Mitchell
1994	W.K. Jewell
1996	N.W. Orchard
1998	J.R. Jarratt
1999	A. Roberts
2000	R. Caple
2001	T.E. Sparrow
2002	P. Sleeman
2003	R.A. Ellis
2004	K.L. Woolcock

When meetings were held at the school no alcoholic refreshments could be offered because it was a Methodist foundation. As the numbers of the lodge grew and meetings grew more frequent it became necessary to find an alternative meeting place. As a result in June 1957 the lodge moved, joining with the Phoenix Lodge, to become tenants of the Fortitude Lodge in Union Place, before moving to new premises in Cyril Road in 1972.

Above - 2003 - 04 First XV
Back row: O. Munn, B. Pollard, M. Lockwood, B. Ackner,
W. Doble Middle row: B. Peet, C. Stein, E. Osman, T.
Somers, T. Swingewood, W. Thompson, E. Dawson
Front row: G. Stickney, W. Charlton, G. Trebilcock, J. Healey
(captain), Mr G.C. Whitmore, D. Hewett, A. Boyd,
J. Tresidder

Left - A wide range of music is studied and performed at
the school among all ages

Writing for the former pupils' newsletter, Matthew Lovatt stated that he was 'eager to continue the excellent work done by my predecessor, Russell Hollins, developing and extending the opportunities for pupils to participate in a wide range of activities both sporting and non-sporting …The school has a wonderful heritage, which I think we should draw upon and celebrate'[9].

Sporting successes continue, both among students and former pupils. Tom Parker was selected to play for the under-18 England rugby team in 2001, and later presented his England shirt to the school, Tom Swingewood was selected to play for the under-16 England team and in 2004, Jamie Tresidder and Will Thompson were invited to play for the under-18 England Presidents XV against a Gloucestershire Schools' side. Rob Thirlby played for England in the Rugby World Seven-a-side Competition in Argentina. Despite a disappointing tournament for England, a *Daily Telegraph* correspondent wrote: 'Whatever Rob Thirlby achieves in

The school continues to have excellent academic results. Among the successful A-level pupils in August 2004 were twins Chloe and Frances Rickard with seven A grades between, pictured here with their parents

his future career he should never forget the night he dumped Jonah Lomu to score a try that helped prevent an embarrassing week-end for England'[10]. In cricket Laura Harper was selected for the England team's tour to New Zealand in 2000. Ben Ainslie's success continues in sailing: having won a silver medal in the Olympics in Atlanta in 1996, he went on to win gold in Sydney and Athens, adding to the sailing gold won in the 1972 Munich Olympics by Christopher Davies.

Over the last few years a new form of A Level has been introduced, taking some of the pressure off the final exams, while I.C.T. was taught for the first time at G.C.S.E. level. In addition, there has been a move to emphasise vocational style education with yet more educational changes on the horizon.

In the school's 125-year history much has changed, though at the same time various aspects have continued, like the school magazine and the debating society, transforming through many different guises. Other aspects appear to be cyclical: 'Truro College' has re-emerged in a new form, as the Sixth Form College at Gloweth. It is clear that many of the issues that concern the school are the same as they were in 1880 - producing a quality education for students from a wide range of backgrounds. 'Matters long dreamt of'[11] have come to fruition and more continue to be planned, while Truro School continues to be 'the centre of light and learning to many...'[12], reflected in the numerous achievements and accomplishments of all those connected with the school.

Famous Former Pupils

Among the numerous former pupils of the school there are those who have risen to the top in their chosen career.

Religion

Despite Truro School being a Methodist foundation it has educated pupils from all faiths, and former pupils include a Buddhist monk, two Anglican bishops, the Right Reverend J.W. Hunkin and the Right Reverend Vernon Nicholls (1929-1934), Bishop of Sodor and Man, Reverend Michael Bordeaux, a director of Keston College and a recognised authority on the modern Russian Church, Reverend N. Wooldridge assistant secretary of the Methodist Conference, as well as two former headmasters, Burrell and Creed, holding the position of Vice-President of the Methodist Conference.

Joseph Hunkin (1887-1953), later Bishop of Truro, was a pupil at Truro College from 1896 to 1903. His father, Joseph Hunkin, a shipbroker, ship owner and coal merchant of Truro, was 'a very old type of 'Glory' Methodist who needed little provocation to start evangelising – somewhat or much to the embarrassment of his son' but 'the Hunkins were kind good people with a strong tendency to be unconventional' who lived in The Parade, Truro; which made it '...possible for J.W.H. to enter the school grounds by climbing over the hedge off the back lane'[1], but it was not long before he was stopped from doing this. The family enjoyed spending time on the river, which was reflected at school with Hunkin mentioned for swimming but little other sport in school magazines. During a swimming race in the Carrick Roads, '...Hunkin and Nicholls became once or twice apparently hopelessly entangled in seaweed, but persisted with indomitable determination'[2]. After Mr Vinter had

retired 'he told some of us that Hunkin was the only boy he had come across who seemed to have knowledge before it was taught to him'[3]. He appears to have had affection for his old school, leading him to write the words to the school song in 1907.

Hunkin preached his first sermon as a Wesleyan local preacher at Tresillian, but it was suggested that 'Hunkin's preaching was not judged to be good enough for him to be trained for the Wesleyan ministry'[4]. He had won several academic prizes while at Truro, and was awarded the Caius Greek Testament prize when at Cambridge studying natural sciences and theology.

During the First World War he had served as a chaplain to the 29th Division of the Royal Artillery. In 1916 he wrote back to the school, from Cape Helles in the Dardanelles

I have now been here eleven days. It is a place of great natural beauty, and the climate has been delightful. I had a bathe on Christmas Day after my morning's round of services. To-day, however, it has been considerably colder, as a north wind is blowing. My work as Chaplain takes me round to half the batteries on the Peninsula. Generally I walk, though sometimes I get a horse for part of the way. I think I know practically all the 29th Division batteries now. They are generally well concealed. To-day I took services in four different places, and buried ten poor fellows in one grave. The Turks get us both from Achi Baba and from Asia. "Asiatic Annie" strafes the beaches, and "Quick Dick" has been a special nuisance. But what everyone loathes most of all are the bombs dropped by Taubes. One section of our line is held by the French, and my opinion of the French has gone up by leaps and bounds. They are so thorough and efficient in so many little ways. There can be no doubt but that a situation like this tends to make a man more thoughtful, and to open his eyes to things he had never paid attention to before[5].

By July 1916 he had moved to France, where he was awarded a Military Cross in 1917; the *West*

Briton ten years later recorded that 'he displayed the utmost bravery at Manchy-le-Preaux, near Arras. Three hundred wounded men lay in cellars there during a terrific bombardment in 1917, and Mr Hunkin faced indescribable dangers to take drinks and smokes to the suffering men'[6]. Writing to the school in July 1918, he had been appointed Senior Chaplain, and had gained a bar to his Military Cross, but was suffering from the effects of gas. On demobilisation he was awarded an O.B.E. and was appointed Dean to his old college of Gonville and Caius in Cambridge. Hunkin taught Archie Marshall at Cambridge, who was at Truro College from 1911 to 1917. Marshall received an unexpected visit from Vinter in his rooms at Cambridge who was pleased that he found him working and was joined by Hunkin, who had climbed up to his rooms to encourage him to attend the services in the College Chapel.

Without doubt Mr Vinter was very proud of Hunkin but, say, during the twenties he had misgivings concerning his belief or possibly lack of belief. He told me privately that he had pushed Hunkin up into a corner and had asked him 'Do you believe in the Resurrection?' and had received the answer 'I believe in the fact of the Resurrection. ...When it was being rumoured that Hunkin was to be appointed Bishop of Truro the rank and file of Anglican laity assumed that he was a High Churchman. This was only because Methodists who became Anglicans tended to be High[7].

However his Methodist background gave him a sympathetic view to the religious situation in Cornwall, where Methodism was still a strong influence. 'Hunkin knew the Methodist position and he was able to work to make the Church of England acceptable to the Cornish. He was able to achieve more in the County Council, in producing agreed syllabuses for religious education than had been possible before'[8]. He was appointed Archdeacon of Coventry and Rector of Rugby in 1927, as well as being a fellow, dean and tutor of Gonville and Caius College, and chaplain to the King. He was consecrated Bishop of Truro in 1935, which he held until his death in 1950.

Entertainment

Among the former pupils who have been involved in the television and film industry the most well known are those who have appeared in front of the camera. However behind the scenes, James Hawes, has a documentary career in TV and film while Matthew Davidge, is a writer and producer in movie business in Los Angeles. Tom Salmon (1933-39) was television manager of B.B.C. South West[9].

Robert Shaw (1927 –1978) lived for several years in Tresillian, and went to school in Ladock before going to Truro School from 1939 to 1945, where he became head prefect in his final year.

Robert Alexander Shaw's father envisioned an Oxford destiny for his son, but Robert's eyes saw a different – We, privileged to know him ahead of the wider public, saw a young actor of unique ability. His Mark Anthony, played when he was just seventeen, compared favourably with the performances of the most experienced Shakespearean actors of the day. At university selection time, like so many of us, Shaw went up to Oxford for the entry examinations. Oxford was not lined up in his sights, but as fine a scholar as he was, pride forbade failure. There were six papers, spread out over three days. After performing brilliantly in the first five he adopted the famous advice, which he surely heard many times, before and after – 'to thine own self be true' – and walked away from the sixth and final paper. Honour and duty satisfied, he returned home. After heart-to-heart talks and soul searching, Robert's father at last accepted that his son would be an actor. Robert attended the Royal Academy of Dramatic Art, where his heart had been all along, instead of Oxford, and lived out a glorious, but far too brief career[10].

Film roles included: Quint in *Jaws* (1975), Red Grant in *From Russia with Love* (1963), Doyle Lonnegan in *The Sting* (1973), Henry VIII in *A Man for All Seasons* (1966) – a performance noted for 'its verbal dagger as well as for its physical swagger'[11].

John Rhys Davies

John Rhys-Davies
attended Truro School from 1953 to 1963, and was head prefect in his final year. While at school he appeared in several school plays including Ulysses in *Troilus and Cressida* in which he 'gave a very fine performance with memorable moments, only occasionally spoiled by unprovoked shouting…Shakespeare gave him the lines and Davies made much of them'[12]. The following year he took the title role in Ben Jonson's *Volpone*:

The Old Fox. The part has been associated in our time with a Very Great Actor Indeed, and it is a thankless task for an amateur to have to approach it in such circumstances. I have no hesitation in judging Davies' reading of Volpone in many ways the truer of the two. He hadn't the massive vocal range, or the comic gifts, or the flawless articulation of the great man, but he had the fertile brain, the restless energy and the suggestion of horse-power in reserve which mark the character, and something else which the great man lacks: a detachment from himself which is essential to his role as critic of the society of which he is at once the victim and the scourge[13].

Film and television roles include: Sallah in *Raiders of the Lost Ark* (1981) and *Indiana Jones and the Last Crusade* (1989), General Leonid Pushkin in *The Living Daylights* (1987), Gimli and Treebeard in *Lord of the Rings* (2001-2003), Vasco Rodrigues in *Shogun* (1980) and Macro in *I, Claudius* (1976).

Nigel Terry left Truro School in July 1963 to study at the Central School of Speech and Drama. He appeared in several school plays, his most notable being in the role of Joxer in *Juno and the Paycock*.

In this part of the Paycock's [played by A.A.F. Cameron] boon companion, Terry, with his sprightly gait, his elfish ear-to-ear grin, his exquisite sense of timing, his precise and eloquent hand gestures, won a large share of the audience's praise, and it was well deserved. His, perhaps, was the outstanding individual performance; but it was not in any sense a selfish one. His teamwork with Cameron was a delight and but one example of the spirit of co-operation which marked the production as a whole[14].

As well as many roles in theatre and television, his film roles also include: John in *The Lion in Winter* (1968), King Arthur in *Excalibur* (1981), and Archeptolemus in *Troy* (2004)

Nigel Terry

In addition to the stage and screen there have been successes in music, including *Ian Little* (1966-71) who was the first organ scholar at the school and became the youngest Cathedral organist at Coventry.

Benjamin Luxon attended Truro School from 1948 to 1955 before studying at the Guildhall School of Music in London. An internationally renowned baritone, he was closely associated with the English Opera Group early in his career, and made his debut at Covent Garden with them in 1972. In 1971 he was chosen by Britten to sing the title role in his television opera *Owen Wingrule*. He has appeared with the English National Opera in roles such as Falstaff, and as Eugene Onegin at the Metropolitan Opera in New York and La Scala in Milan[15].

Alan Opie, also a renowned baritone, was at Truro School from 1956 to 1963 before studying at the Guildhall School of Music in London and the London Opera Centre. His career began with the English National Opera where was principal baritone. As well singing all over the world in operas, concerts and recitals, he has gained a successful recording career and won two Grammies. Among the operas he has performed are *The Magic Flute, The Barber of Seville, Falstaff, Madame Butterfly, Cosi Fan Tutte, Peter Grimes* and *La Boheme*[16].

Roger Taylor, of the internationally famous rock band Queen, came to Truro School in 1960 after the closure of Truro Cathedral School. Before learning the guitar and drums, the first instrument that he learned was the ukulele; by 1966 he was drumming for a popular band 'The Reaction'.

Roger Taylor (copyright PA/EMPICS)

Benjamin Luxon

When he left Truro School in 1968, to pursue a career in dentistry, he moved to London to study biology at the London Hospital Medical College. Soon after he joined the band Smile, led by Brian May. By 1971, the idea of dentistry having been long abandoned, Smile was renamed Queen and the line-up was completed by John Deacon and Freddie Mercury[17].

Business

'At the turn of the century, in one of those coincidences that sometimes happen, there were three boys here who were to crown their careers in Business, Commerce and Banking by being awarded knighthoods'[18]; Sir Sydney Parkes, C.B.E. (1893-93), who had a distinguished career in banking, Sir George Chrstopher (1901-05), chairman and managing director of the Union Castle Steamship Company and president of the British Chamber of Shipping, and Sir John Pascoe (1903-08) was director of British Timkin-Spratton. This group of illustrious business knights was joined in 2001 by Sir Brian Williamson, who, at the time, was chairman and director of the London International Financial Futures and Options Exchange. Other former pupils who have made their name in business include G.W. Lobb, who became director of the British Cotton Industry Research Association, Roy Orford, who was a manager with the U.K. Atomic Energy Authority, R.S. Nicholls who was president of the board of Alka Seltzer and James Modrell who was transport manager with I.C.I.[19]. Paul Myners (1956-66) is presently chairman of Marks & Spencer, as well as an adviser to the Chancellor of the Exchequer and chairman of the *Guardian* and *Observer* newspapers[20].

Public Affairs

Among those holding public office today, or working in public affairs are Mark Prisk, Conservative M.P. for Hertford and Stortford, and Matthew Taylor, Liberal Democrat M.P. for Truro and St Austell, who attended Treliske for a year. Dr David Menhennett (1940-47) held the position of Librarian of the House of Commons. Recently Nigel Heywood was appointed British ambassador to Estonia[21].

From a much earlier time, ***Sir Archie Marshall, Q.C.*** (1911-17) became a high court judge in1959; 'he was believed to be only the third Cornishman in history to have been elevated to the High Court'[22]. The same year he received a knighthood. In 1963 he presided over the trial of Stephen Ward; 'a case made even more unpleasant by the complicated and unsavoury nature of the evidence and Stephen

Ward's eventually successful suicide during the course of the summing up'[23]. His obituary concluded that 'the secret of his greatness and of his wisdom was his essential simplicity, a quality of mind implanted by the indelible impressions of childhood'[24].

David Penhaligon (1944-1986) described as a 'Liberal politician of good sense, charm and promise'[25] was at Truro School from 1953 to 1961.

David Penhaligon (copyright PA/EMPICS)

While at school he was involved in the second XI football team and took an interest in political debates. He was joined the Young Liberals while still at school and took part in school mock elections. He became M.P. for Truro in 1974, becoming a Liberal parliamentary spokesman and later spokesman for energy and industry. He was known for his sense of humour and had the 'common touch'. Re-elected in 1983, Penhaligon was in favour of closer links to the Social Democratic Party. His career was cut short when just before Christmas in 1986 he was killed in a car accident. At the time of his death he had the largest majority on any Liberal M.P. Tipped as a future leader of his party, it was commented that 'he behaved privately as he did in a television studio, and the integrity of that image was something which was generally recognised'[26].

Armed Forces

In addition to the numerous former pupils who fought in both World Wars, the Armed Services have provided careers for several who have risen to prominence around the world. Air Commodore Theodore de Lange C.B.E., D.F.C., who was at the school from 1926 to 1932, served in the New Zealand Air Force. Brigadier General G.R. Gilpin, C.B.E., M.C. 'made a reputation in 1942, by building 'Gilpin's Road' in Burma, with the Royal Engineers over the space of ten weeks'[27]. Dr Douglas Eddy was awarded the Military Cross while serving with the R.A.M.C. from 1942 to 1946, and slightly later Colonel R.A. Preedy, O.B.E. was commander of the 29th Light Regiment Royal Artillery. In 1978 Lieutenant Glen Tilsley was awarded the Air Force Cross for commanding a helicopter rescue operation off the Oil Rig 'Orion'. In the Eighties Squadron Leader G.M. Sharpe of the R.A.F. had spent 2 1/2 years on loan to the Royal Malaysian Air Force and 3 years in Saudi Arabia. Lieutenant Commander John Paton was commanding officer of H.M.S. Dulverton, a Royal Navy mine countermeasure ship[28].

Sport

In recent years, as sport has become increasingly professional a growing number of former pupils have made sport their careers Ben Ainslie has gained Olympic honours in sailing, while Laura Harper has been selected for the England cricket team, Rob Thirlby plays for the England rugby sevens team and golfer Philip Rowe has played for the British Walker cup team[29]. Christopher Davies won gold in the 1972 Olympics in the Flying Dutchman sailing class though his medal ceremony was overshadowed by the terrorist incident that marred the games in Munich. Michael Adams, 'nicknamed Spiderman for his intriguing chess strategies', British Champion and World Champion in rapid-play chess (games which take about 30 minutes), narrowly missed out winning the World Championships held in July 2004[30]. Norman

Laura Harper

Croucher, after a railway accident in which he lost both his lower legs, has had a remarkable mountaineering career, including climbing peaks in the Himalayas, Alps and Peruvian mountain range[31].

John Kendall-Carpenter (1926–1990) attended Truro School from 1939 to 1943. He left school to join the Fleet Air Arm before going up to Exeter College, Oxford. After graduating from Oxford, he

John Kendall-Carpenter

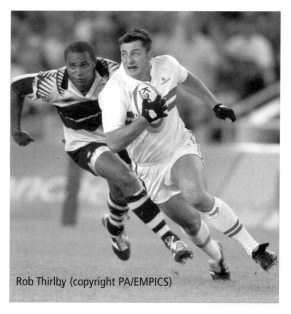

Rob Thirlby (copyright PA/EMPICS)

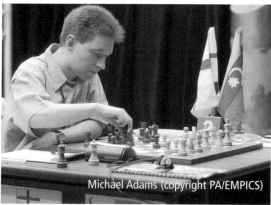

Michael Adams (copyright PA/EMPICS)

Ben Ainslie (copyright PA/EMPICS)

began his teaching career in 1951 as geography master at Clifton College, Bristol. Ten years later he took up the position of headmaster of Cranbrook School in Kent, where after nine years he moved on to become headmaster of Eastbourne College. His final school was Wellington in Somerset, and during his headmastership there he chaired the Boarding Schools Association between 1981 and 1983.

Parallel to teaching, Kendall-Carpenter also had a successful rugby career, both on and off the pitch. While at school he does not appear to have played for the first team but when at Oxford he gained three rugby Blues. He made 28 appearances for the Cornwall County team as well as playing for the Barbarians, Penzance-Newlyn and Bath, and captained every team he played for. During the 1950s he was selected for England, playing 23 times as a back-row forward, and captaining the team on several occasions. 'He was a man of immense energy and stamina who managed to devote an enormous amount of time to the cause of rugby football… one of the great rugby football administrators of his day'[32]. In 1980-81 he was President of the Rugby Football Union, and was later elected to the International Rugby Board while President of the Schools R.F.U. Having gained widespread respect from the other countries making up the I.R.B., he was elected chairman of the steering committee that organised the first Rugby World Cup, held in New Zealand in 1987. He was in charge of organising the 1991 World Cup, until his sudden death in May 1990[33]. He kept his ties with Cornish rugby, holding the position of President of the Cornish R.F.U. in 1985.

John Kendall-Carpenter continued his connection with his old school throughout his life. He was chairman of the London branch of the Old Boys' Association in 1953 and 1964, and later became a vice-president. He returned to the school in 1980 for the centenary celebrations and again in 1988 when he provided a witty and engaging speech as the guest speaker at the school's speech day. In 1995 the first rugby match between Truro School and Wellington School was played, competing for the Kendall-Carpenter Cup given in his memory[34].

Appendix

Headmasters

1880 – 1887	George Owen Turner
1887 – 1889	Thomas Jackson
1889 – 1921	Herbert William Vinter
1921 – 1946	Egbert Hockey Magson
1946 – 1959	Albert Lowry Creed
1959 – 1986	Derek Burrell
1986 - 1992	Russell Hobbs
1992 – 1993	Brian Jackson (Acting Head)
1993 - 2001	Guy Dodd
2001 -	Paul Smith

Second Masters

1880 -1881	W. Vincent
1881 – 1883?	F. M. Facer
1883 – 1890	H. W. Vinter
1890	J. H. Harper
1890 - 1894	E. G. Gane
1894 - 1897	G. H. Hunter
1897 - 1898	H. Wilkinson
1901 – 1904	J. M. V. Stead
1904 -1908	H. B. Mills
1908 – 1909	H. Bromley
1909 – 1910	A. F. Young
1910	H. V. Lowe
1910 - 1921	S. B. Wilson
1921 - 1960	E. B. Willday
1960 – 1968	W.E.B. Worthington
1968 – 1974	C.F. Wilkes
1974 – 1978	A.J. Tonkin
1978 – 1990	E.J. Taylor
1990 – 1994	B. Jackson
1992 -	S. Price
	(Joint Deputy Head in 1993-4)
1999 -	Mrs P.A. Harris
	(Joint Deputy Head)

Headmasters of Treliske

1936 – 1961	T. Stratton
1961 – 1988	A.W. Ayres
1988 – 2003	R.L. Hollins
2003 – 2004	Mrs J. Grassby (Acting Head)
2004 -	M.J. Lovett

Chairmen of the School Governors 1904 – 2004

1904 – 1921	Sir George Smith
1921 – 1948	Col. Stanley Smith
1948 – 1965	Graham B. Smith
1965 – 1973	Rev. R.H. Luke
1973 – 1973	Rev. D.J. Hubery
1973 – 1989	J. Bedford Daniel
1989 – 1992	Prof. J.C. Dancy
1992 - 2003	J.R. Heath
2003 -	J. Baxter

Chaplains

1927 – 1930	Rev. J. R. Temple
1930 – 1933	Rev. J. R. S. Hutchinson
1933 – 1934	Rev. H. R. Wilkinson
1934	Rev. G. L. Cocks
1935 – 1937	Rev Clifford Buckroyd
1937 – 1938	Rev. K. E. Woodruff
1938 – 1941	Rev. John H Wroe
1941 – 1943	Rev. L. E. Hickin
1943 – 1944	Rev. L. E. White
1944	Rev. T. Harris
1947 – 1950	Rev. N. Richardson
1950 – 1954	Rev. V. V. Cooper
1954 – 1960	Rev. A. G. Loosemore
1960 – 1964	Rev. Dr. J. Mole
1964 – 1973	Rev. T. B. Coleman
1973 – 1984	Rev. B. G. Holland
1984 – 1989	Rev. R. Wood
1989 – 1997	Rev. J. Johnson
1997 – 2003	Mr R. J. Buley
2003 -	Rev. A. de Gruchy

Bursars

1938 - 1939	H.V. Smith
1939 – 1958	Beecher Williams
1958 – 1979	H. J. Appleton
1980 – 1998	G. R. Oram
1999 -	A. M. Jones

Chairmen of Truro School Former Pupils' Association

1922	H.W. Vinter
1923	J.A. Jennings
1924	W.C. Smith
1925	W. Hearle
1926	T. Wickett
1927	J.I. Higgins
1928	E.S. Beard

1929	E.P. Adams	1981	T.C. Hoskin
1930	H.T. Pearson	1982	R.L.J. Goddard
1931	W.R. Lobb	1983	D.W. Downing
1932	F.W. Truscott	1984	R.H.T. Moore
1933	W.A. Jennings	1985	R.G. Worsley-White
1934	E.S. Vincent	1986	H. Berryman
1935	R.B. Webb	1987	R. Woodward
1936	B.O. Mitchell	1988	C.B. Rowe
1937	J.H. Rosewarne	1989	W.P. Eathorne
1938	L. Bellingham	1990	F.M. Mitchell
1939-41	W.F. Jewell	1991	T.J. Page
1942	F.G. Beel	1992	C.C. Tidball
1943-44	J.G. Barrett	1993	C. Harding
1945	H.A. Philp	1994	D.L. Rogers
1946	Beecher Williams	1995	G.P.G. Rowe
1947	W.C. Argall	1996	W.J. Harris
1948	L.A. Dotson	1997	T. Sperring
1949	L.A. Dotson	1998	Ms S. Smitham
1950	S. Mitchell	1999	J. Dale
1951	W.T.H. Rowse	2000	D.F. Castling
1952	W.A.J. Davey	2001	D.F. Castling
1953	G.L.W. Beards	2002	S.J.H. Floyd
1954	H.H. Mitchell	2003	S.J.H. Floyd
1955	A.J. Tonkin	2004	G. Murdoch
1956	H.D. Eddy		
1957	H.O. Rule		
1958	D.S. Vage		

***Chairmen of the Truro Former Pupils'
Association London Branch, 1924 - 1988***

1959	T.E.F. Mutton	1924	A.L. Potts
1960	T.H. Hicks	1925	R.S. Gledhill
1961	J.S. Vincent	1926	J.H. Way
1962	T.E. Vincent	1927-35	Branch dormant
1963	W.H.E.A. Thomas	1936	R.S. Gledhill
1964	P.W. Boggia	1937	L.F. Fairchild
1965	G.J. Hendra	1938	L.F. Fairchild
1966	D. Lloyd	1939-45	G. White
1967	J.C.B. Daniel	1946	F.K. Exell
1968	C.F. Wilkes	1947	F.K. Exell
1969	S.G. Heyworth	1948	R.H. Rowse
1970	F.W. Luck	1949	R.H. Rowse
1971	H.J. Appleton	1950	W.A. Boggia
1972	E.J. Collins	1951	D.L. Simmons
1973	P.M.N. Scantlebury	1952	L.A. Dotson
1974	N.J. Mutton	1953	C.C. Bennett
1975	J.E. Kerkin	1954	A.T.A. Dixon
1976	D.B. Gripe	1955	T.H. Willoughby
1977	W.I. Murdoch	1956	W.J.C. Delbridge
1978	P. Tremewan	1957	I.S. Story
1979	A.J. Tonkin & D.A.G. Dunstan	1958	W.M. Tresidder
1980	D.A.G. Dunstan	1959	E.G. Thomas

1960	A.D. Nicholls
1961	M. Lewis
1962	A.E. Joyce
1963	R.L. Sweet
1964	M.C. Eastree
1965	D.G. Salt
1966	R.C. Crewes
1967	R.B. Shepherd
1968	J. Kendall-Carpenter
1969	I.F. Goodhand
1970	W.J. Harris
1971	E.W. Gillies
1972	P.H. Williams
1973	T.L. Rundell
1974	W.J.C. Delbridge
1975	A.W. Davis
1976	P.G. Roberts
1977	C.D. Hore
1978	W.J. Harris
1979	R.L. Sweet
	& J. Kendall-Carpenter
1980	R.C. Orford
1981	J. Daniel
1982	P.H. Williams
1983	M. Carreras
1984	K.W. Aitken
1985	R.W. Dean
1986	I.F. Kolbé
1987	M. Kearney
1988	C.J. York

Head Prefects since 1896

1896	C.L. Bryant
1897	R.J.P. Julian
1898	A.M. Williams
1899	A.M. Williams
1900	J.L. Kitto
1901	J.L. Kitto
1902	H.M. Nicholls
1903	H.M. Nicholls
1904	J.W. Hunkin
1905	T.J. Rickard
1906	H. Mitchell
1907	A.L. Harding
1908	A.L. Harding
1909	C.W. Tregenza
1910	W.J. Gilpin & W.T. Gregor
1911	W.H. Tregea & W.A. Tregenza
1912	J.K. Peel

1913	G.R. Gilpin
1914	F.E. Gilpin
1915	A.E. Tregea
1916	L.P. Ingram
1917	H.W. Chegwidden
	& R.A. Roberts
1918	W.F. Rogers
1919	R.H. Eagan
1920	F.K. Exell
1921	F.K. Exell
1922	R.J. Pearce
1923	C.D. Webb
1924	A.B. Hamson & R.H.R. Tregunna
1925	W.W. Thomas
1926	T.S. Magson
1927	A.F. Pownall
1928	J.D. Dale Green
1929	H. Kent
1930	G.W. Lobb
1931	D.R.R. Robinson
1932	D.B. McKinney
1933	J.H.H. Magson
1934	J.H.H. Magson
1935	J.F. Jory
1936	P.O. Brown
1937	D.R. Worthington
1938	B. Beckerleg
1939	C.G.L. Beveridge
1940	T.W.N. Beasant
1941	P.C. Pawlyn
1942	F.R. Modrell
1943	J.C. Faull
1944	E.J.D. Warne
1945	R.A. Shaw
1946	I.F. Goodhand
1947	D.E. Goodhand
1948	T.M. Stross
1949	H.D. Richards
1950	M.E.C. Drew
1951	W.J. Dale
1952	W.P. Stephens
1953	L.J.J. Kendall
1954	R.E.T. Biddick
1954	R.C. Grime
1955	P. Underwood
1956	C.H. Phillips
1957	M.A. Fido
1957	M.T. Hardy
1958	G.B. Haycock

1959	C.R. Douglas	1913	G.R. Gilpin
1960	J.W. Daniel	1914	G.R. Gilpin
1961	N. Tonkin	1915	A.E. Tregea
1962	D.N. McKirgan	1916	A. Manners
1963	H.J. Davies and R.B. Williamson	1917	R.A. Roberts
1964	S.P. Sylvester	1918	A.C. Rowe
1965	A.G. Watts	1919	P. Williams
1966	T.M. Warne	1920	F.K. Exell
1967	A.M. Willmett	1921	L.H. Hosken
1968	D.K. James	1922	F.W. Barlow
1969	T.P. Tonkin	1923	J.D Couch
1970	C. Hoare	1924	A.B. Hamson
1971	R.J. Bulley	1925	J.R. Barnard
1972	A.D.F. Brookes and R.M. Cottle	1926	W.W. Thomas
1973	W. Trelawny	1927	J.D. Buckle
1974	P. Eddy	1928	A.F. Pownall
1975	N.M. Pritchard- Davies	1929	E.M. Brown
1976	D.C. Pencheon	1930	H. Kent
1977	C. Tozer and R. Fairburn	1931	G.W. Lobb
1978	A.Q. Peck	1932	J .C. Nicholls
1979	J. Clift	1933	S.E. Gourd
1980	N.P.B. Morton	1934	J.H.H. Magson
1981	T.M. Chatterton	1935	A.L. Andrew
		1936	J.F. Jory

Cricket Captains

1883	E. Boyns	1937	S.H. Lobb
1886	E. Vine	1938	R.L. Sweet
1890	H. Vivian	1939	I.D.K. Halkerston
1892	W. Rowe	1940	A.T. Visick
1893	G.H. Brenton	1941	A.T. Visick
1894	E. Rowe	1942	D.W.H. Norris
1895	E. Rowe	1943	W.S. Hickson
1896	J.F. Shipham	1944	T.K. Vivian
1897	J.F. Shipham	1945	T.K. Vivian
1898	R.G. Hosking	1946	C.E.P. Stephens
1899	F.W. Kendall	1947	W.B. Faull
1900	M.E. Nicholls	1948	T.W. Cory
1901	H.S. Prideaux	1949	T.W. Cory
1902	H.M. Nicholls	1950	M.E.C. Drew
1903	H.M. Nicholls	1951	A.E. Murton
1904	W.S. Allport	1952	W.M. Buzza
1905	T.J. Rickard	1953	L.J. Kendall
1906	E.J.P. Burling	1954	R.E.T. Biddick
1907	A.S. Whitworth	1955	A.S. Mumford
1908	A.S Whitworth	1956	J.M. Boulden
1909	W.J. Gilpin	1957	R.G. Barber
1910	W. Manners	1958	R.C. Harvey
1911	H.C. Whitworth	1959	C.T. Moore
1912	G.R. Gilpin	1960	R. Hatham
		1961	R.H. Blackburn

1962	M.A. Woolcock		1895-96	F. Rowe
1963	P. Milton		1896-97	F. Rowe
1964	C.J. Hooson		1897-98	J.F. Shipham
1965	J.M. Platts		1898-99	R.G. Hosking
1966	C. Rashleigh		1899-1900	F.W. Kendall
1967	P.D. Hooson		1900-01	H.S. Prideaux
1968	D. Marshall		1901-02	H.M. Nicholls
1969	T.P. Tonkin		1902-03	H.M. Nicholls
1970	R.J. Bulley		1903	H.M. Nicholls
1971	R.J. Bulley		1904	R.W. Henwood
1972	R.N. Mitchell		1905	T.J. Rickard
1973	W.P. Berryman		1906	H. Mitchell
1974	M. J. Trewhella		1907	C.W. Tregenza
1975	S.J.H. Floyd		1908	C.W. Tregenza
1976	S.J.H. Floyd		1909	W.J. Gilpin
1977	R. Lang		1910	W.H. Tregea
1978	G.C. Stephens		1911	W.A. Tregenza
1979	C.P. Triniman		1912	G.R. Gilpin
1980	T.M. Chatterton		1913	G.R. Gilpin
1981	M.E. Barlow		1914	F.E. Gilpin
1982	T.J. Manhire		1915	A.E. Tregea
1983	M.G. Phillips		1916	R.A. Roberts
1984	M.W. Yates		1917	R.A. Roberts
1985	P.G. Phillips		1918	W.F. Rogers
1986	S.R. Peters		1919	F.K. Exell
1987	J.A. Johnston		1920	L.H. Hosken
1988	D.J.F. Griffiths		1921	P. Pearce
1989	A. Symons		1922	F.W.M. Hearle
1990	T. Perkins		1923	F.W. M. Hearle
1991	T. Perkins		1924	A.B. Hamson
1992	J. Hurrell		1925	F.W. Emmett
1993	R. Atkins		1926	J.D. Buckle
1994	S. Holman		1927	A.F. Pownall
1995	R. Harmer		1928	H. Kent
1996	T. Sharp		1929	H. Kent
1997	T. Sharp		1930	D.B. McKinney
1998	J. Price		1931	A.J. Tonkin
1999-2000	B. Price		1932	J. Baron
2000-01	O. Turnbull		1933	J.H.H. Magson
2001-02	D. Pollard		1934	J.H.H. Magson
2002-03	T. Glover		1935	J.F. Jory
			1936	H.W. Polkinghorne
			1937	P.O. Brown

Football Captains

1882-83	E. Boyns		1938	R.H. Venning
1887-88	C.V. Wills		1939	T.W.N. Beasant
1891-92	W.H. Thomas		1940	W.G. Luke
1892–93	H. Vivian		1941	T. Beasant
1893–94	G.H. Brenton		1942	P.C. Pawlyn
1894-95	E. Rowe		1943	F.R. Moddrel

1944	T.K. Vivian		**Rugby Captains**	
1945	T.K. Vivian		1882	E. Boyns
1946	I.F. Goodhand		1931	D.B. McKinney
1947	W.B. Faull		1932	D.B. McKinney
1948	H.D. Richards		1933	J.H.H. Magson
1949	H.D. Richards		1934	J.H.H. Magson
1950	M.E.C. Drew		1935	W.B. Faull
1951	D.P. Badcock		1936	D.I.M. Robins
1952	A.M. Harvey		1937	R.L. Sweet
1953	R.E.T. Biddick		1938	R.L. Sweet
1954	R.E.T. Biddick		1939	G. Sawle
1966	S.J. Passmore		1940	T. Beasant
1967	A. Westcott		1941	P.C. Pawlyn
1968	A. Westcott		1942	V.K. Nance
1969	J.N. Francis		1943	V.K. Nance
1970	K.C. Benney		1944	T.K. Vivian
1971	S.W. Harris		1945	I. Goodhand
1972	P. Mewton		1946	W.B. Faull
1973	H.T. Nicholls		1947	H.D. Richards
1974	N. R. Tregenna		1948	H.D. Richards
1975	S. Harrison		1949	M.E.C. Drew
1976	R. Shore		1950	D.P. Badcock
1977	J.P. Clift		1951	A.M. Harvey & F.J.B. Mumford
1978	J.P. Clift		1952	R.C. Stephens
1979	G. Champion		1953	R.E.T. Biddick
1980	R.M. Smith		1954	A.S. Mumford
1981	C. Keast		1955	P. Underwood
1982	S.P. Watts		1956	J.R. Williams
1983	M. Blomfield		1957	M.T. Hardy
1984	S.J. Richards		1958	C.R. Douglas
1985	S.J. Richards		1959	C.J. Allan
1986	M. Osborne		1960	S.G. Julian & D.A.J. Lord
1987	S. Peters		1961	R.H. Blackburn
1988	S.M. Ashman		1962	D.W. Ellis
1989	R.J. Morse		1963	A.A.F. Cameron
1990	J.R. Venables		1964	J.M. Platts
1991	P.A. Nuttall		1965	J.M. Platts
1992	J. Hurrell		1966	A.G. Hall
1993	S. Richardson		1967	D.K. James
1994	A. Joint		1968	S.J. Nicholas
1995	T. Sharp		1969	M. Potten
1996	T. Sharp		1970	C. Stamper
1997	L. Meza		1971	P.J.W. Shipwright
1998	R. Cairns		1972	S.W. Harris
1999	M. Otty		1973	D. Shipwright
2000	M. Otty		1974	N. Morgan
2001	M. Willmore		1975	S.J.H. Floyd
2002	M. Farmer		1976	C.J. Tozer
2003	T. Glover		1977	D. Morgan

1978	N.C. Hunter
1979	S.H. Lane
1980	T.M. Chatterton
1981	M.E.H. Peck
1982	M.J. Blomfield
1983	S.W. Whitworth
1984	M.R. Little
1985	P.G. Phillips
1986	J.A.N. Pritchard
1987	J.A. Johnston
1988	I.M. Boase
1989	E.W. Folkes
1990	D.R.J. Leslie
1991	M. Johnston
1992	G. Shore
1993	J. Hendy
1994	B. Moore
1995	D. Tinkley
1996	L. Meza
1997	M. MacMahon
1998	B. Price
1999	M. Otty
2001	D. Pollard
2002	D. Pollard
2003	T. Glover
2004	J. Healey

Girls' Hockey Captains

1981	J.A. George
1982	J.A. George
1983	C.L. Woodford
1984	L.J. Pritchard
1985	T. Raymond
1986	A.M. Collins
1987	S.E. Symons
1988	A. Barrington
1989	S. Bates
1990	S. Allsopp
1991	K. Eustace
1992	C. Drew
1993	J. Richardson
1994	S. Atkinson
1995	A. Pritchard
1996	N. Simpson
1997	T. Ryall
1998	K. Barton
1999	C. Leigh
2000	N. Simpson
2001	G. Hyslop

2002	A. Jenkin

Netball Captains

1990	V.J. Howard
1991	K. Eustice
1993	S. Atkinson
1994	E. Lovegrove
1995	F. Allsop
1996	E. James
1997	J. Paull
1998	A. Allen
1999	N. Lay
2000	V.G. Walker
2001	S. Henshall
2002	S. Henshall

War Memorials
Boer War, 1899 - 1903
Champion, W. Lewis
Magor, Martin
Hosking, G. E.

The First World War, 1914 – 1918
Banfield, Cyril Barnes
Banfield, Eldred Cole
Bell, Reginald Milburn
Blamey, William
Brewer, Francis Henry
Brewer, Henry James
Cann, Percy
Collins, Charles Edwin
Crewes, Reginald Charles
Curtis, Tom Cleave
Davies, Leonard
Dreyer, Leslie L.
Ford, William
Friend, Geoffrey Martin
Gill, Reginald Searle
Gilpin, Robert
Gregory, Joseph Glasson
Hicks, Frank Llewellyn
Hill, Wilfred James
Hosking, William Henry
Jacobs, Ronald Frank Perran
James, John Pryor
Julian, Edgar Jenkin
Lawry, William Arthur
Lillecrapp, Jack Dunn
Little, Edwin

Martin, Jabez
Martyn, Marshall Everett
Mawer, William Gerald Hicks
Millard, Harold Austin
Mitchell, Sampson Edgar
Nicholls, Harold Mayne
Oxenberry, John Edward
Parkin, Gilbert Horace Harcourt
Pascoe, Henry Martin
Paynter, John
Pengelly, Frederick
Pryor, Edgar Harry
Richards, Morley Truscott
Richards, William George
Rickard, Henry Cecil
Ridgill, Charles R.
Roberts, George Jewell
Roberts, Thomas Stephen
Seymour, Herbert Alfred
Shafto, John Stanley H.
Spargo, Bertram Donald
Spargo, Loris Stiles
Stevens, Philip Bennett
Thomas, Frank Hender
Walkey, Francis Ashton
Whitburn, Herbert L.
Whitford, Simon Henry
Whitworth, Herbert Clifford
Williams, Frank

The Second World War, 1939 – 1945
Andrew, James Francis
Audley, Derek Dundonald
Baruch, Ernest Theodor Siegmund
Bawden, Reginald V.
Bellingham, Leonard
Bennett, David Robert
Bennett, Richard John
Bennett, R. J. Paul
Blewett, Edward
Brewer, Leslie F.
Cann, Percy Reginald
Clift, Alexander
Clifton, F.A.N.
Crapp, Francis G.
Curties, George A.
Deeble, Robert James
Donahue, Dennis

Drabble, R. Kenneth John
Dunstan, Donald Leslie
Eyles, Peter Raoul
Fittock, Charles M.
Fox, Arthur Herbert
Hackforth, Robert Newton
Hackforth, Samuel Nicholas
Hadley, Ronald
Hawkey, George
Hill, David Samuel
Hodge, Joseph Stanley
Hoskin, Eric Charles
Hosking, Edwin Bennett
Ingham, Richard John
Jewell, John St Aubyn
Kendall, Jack Willoughby
Knapman, William E. Lethbridge
Knight, Christopher T. J. T.
Lander, Charles
Luke, Henry Gordon
Martin, Edwin Bernard
Martin, Henry John
May, Alan Graham
McKay, Robert Hamilton
McLay, Charles Kenneth
Moore, Philip Henry Hugh
Moore, Robert
Pedlar, Clifford Stephen
Penberthy, Ernest James
Penberthy, Paul
Penhaligon, Thomas Edward Jim
Phillips, Denis Robert
Pugh, Evan Gilbert
Senior, John Norman
Smith, John Creese
Stanier, Arnold
Stephens, Frederick
Tallack, John Basil
Thomas, Arthur Cyril
Thomas, Herbert Ronald
Thomas, Ronald A.O.
Tregoning, John Thomas
Treloar, Albert Lewis
Trewhella, Hugh Kingsley
Turnbull, Douglas Elliot
Turnbull, Robert Arthur Felix
Williamson, Peter Macgregor
Wise, Peter C.

Notes

1. 1880 - 1889: 'The Pioneer Years'

1 G.O. Turner, 'History of the School, part 1' Truro College Magazine (T.C.M.), July 1892, 5
2 Ibid, 3
3 T. Shaw, A History of Cornish Methodism p.118 (1967)
4 The History Today Companion to British History (1995) 269-270
5 Royal Cornwall Gazetteer, 23 January 1880
6 V. Acton and B. Acton, A History of Truro: Cathedral City and County Town, volume 2, (2002) pp.13-15
7 From Notes by J.N. Rosewarne, a former pupil 1909-1916
8 M. Tangye, 'The Wesleyan Methodist Relief Fund for the Cornwall District, 1879' Old Cornwall volume 7, 186
9 Turner, 'History of the School, article I', 3
10 Turner, 'History of the School, article II', T.C.M., April 1893, 88
11 Royal Cornwall Gazette, 10 June 1881
12 Turner, 'History of the School, article I', 4.
13 Cornwall Advertiser, Thursday January 23, 1913
14 Turner, 'History of the School, article I', 7
16 Turner, 'History of the School, article II', 87
17 Ibid, 89
18 Royal Cornwall Gazette 10 June 1881
19 N. Baker (ed) Truro School Centenary 1880-1980, (1980) p.5
20 Royal Cornwall Gazette, 10 June 1881
21 Ibid
22 Turner, 'History of the School, article II', 89
23 Kelly's Directory 1883
24 H.W. Vinter, 'History of the School, article III', T.C.M., July 1893, 121
25 From notes made by J.N. Rosewarne, son of Henry Rosewarne.
26 From a letter by T.W.M Darlington, 1994.
27 From a letter by J. McCoskrie, 1955.
28 G.H. Hunter, 'History of the School, article IV', T.C.M., December 1893, 159
29 From notes by J.N. Rosewarne
30 Vinter, 'The History of the School, article III', 122
31 Hunter, 'The History of the School, article IV', 158-9
32 Editorial, T.C.M., July 1892, 1
33 Vinter, 'History of the School, article III', 122
34 Turner, 'The History of the School, article I', 7
35 Ibid, 123
36 Ibid, 160
37 Vinter, 'The History of the School, article III', 123-4
38 Vinter, 'History of the School, article III', 124
39 Hunter, 'History of the School, article IV', 159

2. George Turner

1 H.W. Vinter, Obituary in T.C.M., December 1921, 52
2 West Briton 28 July 1887, 6
3 Vinter in T.C.M., December 1921, 52
4 Old Boys' Dinner report in T.C.M., April 1905, 96

3. Thomas Jackson

1 H.W. Vinter, 'The History of the School, article III' T.C.M., December 1893, 160-1
2 T.C.M., April 1895
3 T.C.M., July 1906
4 T.C.M., December 1924
5 T.C.M., April 1905
6 T.C.M., December 1933

4. 1890 - 1899: The School and the Wider World

1 E.S. Vincent in a letter to GO Vinter, written 20 November 1964
2 T.C.M., December 1895, 60
3 T.C.M., July 1897, 12. G.M. Best, Continuity and Change: A History of Kingswood School 1748-1998 (1998) p.114
4 Best, Continuity and Change pp.114-5
5 T.C.M., July 1897, 12
6 1896 Speech Day
7 T.C.M., July 1894, 45
8 T.C.M., December 1892, 48-9
9 T.C.M., April 1893, 94
10 T.C.M., December 1894, 56
11 T.C.M., April 1893, 94
12 T.C.M., July 1897
13 Sir G.P. Christopher, Through the Years p.24. (At Truro College 1901-1905).
14 T.C.M., July 1892
15 T.C.M., July 1891
16 T.C.M., July 1894,13

17 T.C.M., July 1895
18 G.H. Hunter, 'The History of the School, article V' T.C.M., April 1894, 12
19 Editorial (G.H. Hunter) T.C.M., July 1891, 1
20 T.C.M., December 1894,1
21 Hunter 'The History of the School, article V', 10
22 T.C.M., December 1891, 40
23 T.C.M., July 1894, 43
24 T.C.M., December 1892, 43
25 T.C.M., April 1892, 95
26 T.C.M., December 1894, 69 and 81

5. Herbert Vinter
1 Cambridge Alumni; entered 1879. 1881 census: living 3 Park Terrace, Cambridge with his father and sister as an undergraduate, aged 24.
2 Sir G.P. Christopher, Through the Years pp.24-25
3 Photocopy of a letter to GO Vinter from Sir Archibald Marshall, QC, December 1964. In letter from GO Vinter to Nigel Baker, 9 May 1980
4 From notes by J.N. Rosewarne, at Truro College 1909-1916
5 Letter from E.S. Vincent to G.O. Vinter, 20 November 1964
6 From notes by J. N. Rosewarne
7 Governors' minutes 1904 - 1919
8 Photocopy of a letter to G.O. Vinter from Sir Archibald Marshall, QC, December 1964.
9 T.C.M., July 1930, 43

6. 1900 – 1909: 'High on the Hill with the City below'
1 T.C.M., April 1900, 85
2 Sir G.P. Christopher, Through the Years, pp.24 and 30
3 T.C.M., July 1900, 12
4 T.C.M., April 1900, 86
5 T.C.M., July 1900, 13
6 T.C.M., December 1901, 71-2
7 Letters from Joe Thomas, printed in the T.C.M., April 1900, 105-112
8 Letter from Jack Thomas, printed in the T.C.M., July 1900, 34
9 T.C.M., December 1900, 112
10 T.C.M., December 1902, 77

11 T.C.M., July 1902, 12
12 Ibid, 13
13 T.C.M., December 1900, 112
14 From a report by Tom Wickett in T.C.M., December 1901, 73-4
15 M. Carver, The National Army Museum Book of the Boer War (1999) pp.207-8
16 T. Shaw, A History of Cornish Methodism (1967) p.118
17 Cornwall Advertiser, Thursday January 23, 1913
18 T.C.M., January 1904, 50-1
19 T.C.M., April 1905, 105
20 T.C.M., December 1901
21 From notes by J.N. Rosewarne, at Truro College 1909-1916.
22 T.C.M., December 1909
23 T.C.M., July 1909, 9
24 T.C.M., July 1924, 36
25 T.C.M., April 1910, 113
26 T.C.M., April 1903, 88; December 1904; December 1909, and April 1910, 105

Mrs Opie
1 From notes by J.N. Rosewarne, at Truro College 1909 – 1916.
2 J.N. Rosewarne and C.H. Bray in T.C.M., July 1921, T.C.M., December 1921, 55-56
3 T.C.M., July 1921
4 T.C.M., December 1921, 56
5 T.C.M., July 1923, 8
6 The Truronian, July 1951, 13

7. 1910 - 1919: 'Shoulder to shoulder in war and peace'
1 T.C.M., July 1930 p.43
2 Photocopy attached to letter from GO Vinter, extract from 'a local Truro, Cornwall, paper: "Fifty Years Back"', November 20th 1964.
3 From notes by J.N. Rosewarne, at Truro College 1909-1916.
4 Ibid.
5 T.C.M., December 1914, 43
6 Governors' Minutes, 1910 – 1915, 17 August 1914
7 Governors' Minutes, 1915 – 1923, 17 September 1918
8 Governors' Minutes, 1915 – 1923, 15 December 1915

9   Governors' Minutes, 1915 – 1923, 16 November 1915
10 T.C.M., December 1914 – April 1916
11 T.C.M., July 1915, 4
12 Ibid, 21
13 Ibid, 22
14 T.C.M., December 1916,52-3
15 T.C.M., July 1917, 17
16 Ibid, 99
17 Ibid, 97
18 Ibid, 100
19 Ibid, 6
20 T.C.M., April 1918
21 T.C.M., July 1918
22 Governors' Minutes, 1915 – 1923, 18 January 1915
23 T.C.M., April 1917, 17
24 T.C.M., April 1916, 91
25 T.C.M., December 1917, 65-66
26 T.C.M., December 1918, 44-45
27 From notes by J.N Rosewarne
28 T.C.M., July 1915
29 T.C.M., July 1918, 16
30 T.C.M., July 1917, 24, www.orcadian.co.uk/features/articles/vanguard.htm and Loss of H.M.S. Vanguard - www.gwpda.org/naval/vanguard.htm
31 T.C.M., April 1918, 14-15
32 T.C.M., April 1918, 109-110
33 T.C.M., April 1917
34 T.C.M., December 1918, 1
35 T.C.M., July 1920
36 Governors' Minutes, 1915 – 1923, 12 February 1918

8. 1920 - 1929: 'A New Era Begins'
1   T.C.M., December 1921, 39-40
2   Ibid, 40
3   Ibid, 41
4   West Briton, 1927
5   1924 Inspection Report
6   A.J.P. Taylor, English History 1914 – 1945 (1966) pp.184-5
7   Ibid, p. 211
8   1924 Inspection Report
9   Ibid
10 West Briton, 11 May 1925
11 The Truronian, April 1928, 69

12 T.C.M., July 1922, 29
13 The Truronian, December 1929, 43
14 T.C.M., December 1921, 59-60
15 Ibid, 58-9
16 1928 Speech Day Report
17 The Truronian, March 1928, 81
18 The Truronian, July 1927, 2
19 Ibid, 3
20 Ibid, 5
21 The Truronian, December 1928, 35
22 Western Morning News, 9 June 1927
23 The Truronian, July 1927, 10
24 Truro School Association Minute Book 1924 – 1950: 'Old Truronians, London'.
25 N. Baker, (ed.) Truro School Centenary 1880 – 1980, p.20
26 T.C.M., July 1922, 1
27 T.C.M., April 1922
28 The Truronian, March 1926, 37 - 40
29 T.C.M., July 1922, 29
30 The Truronian, December 1926, 24
31 West Briton, 23 February 1928
32 The Truronian, April 1928, 78-79
33 The Truronian, March 1929, 73-74
34 T.C.M., July 1923, 21-22
35 The Truronian, December 1926, 24

9. E.H. Magson
1   1891 census, from www.ancestry.co.uk
2   T.C.M., December 1921, 35-36
3   The Truronian, December 1961, 5-6
4   Truro School Association Newsletter, February 2000

10. 1930 - 1939: Truro School
1   The Truronian, March 1931, 96-97
2   The Truronian, March 1934, 125-126
3   West Briton, 12 February 1934, and West Briton, 11 July 1935
4   West Briton, 6 March 1934
5   West Briton, 11 July 1935
6   Western Morning News, 27 June 1935
7   The Truronian, March 1932, 74
8   Speech Day Report 1933-34, p.4
9   The Truronian, July 1930, 45
10 Truro School Association Newsletter, February 2000
11 The Truronian, July 1930, 9

12 Speech Day Report 1932-33, p.5
13 The Truronian, July 1960, 29
14 The Truronian, July 1936, 27
15 Speech Day Report 1935-36, p.2
16 John Bridger, at Truro School 1938–1945, in Truro School Association Newsletter, February 2000
17 Punishment Book 1936-1943
18 Speech Day Report 1933-34, p.3
19 The Truronian, April 1937, 129
20 The Truronian, July 1939, 17
21 The Truronian, March 1933, 103
22 The Truronian, July 1934, 9
23 The Truronian, March 1938, 20
24 The Truronian, December 1933, 64
25 Ibid, 98-99
26 The Truronian, December 1936, 66-68
27 Ibid, 80-81
28 Speech Day Report 1937-38, p.7-8
29 Speech Day Report 1938-39, p.8
30 The Truronian, July 1937, 2
31 The Truronian, December 1938, 2-9
32 Speech Day Report 1932-33, pp.10-11
33 Speech Day Report 1937-38, p.4

11. Treliske

1 R. Barrett, Stately Homes in and around Truro (1980)
2 1891 Census, Kenwyn Parish, Folio 30, p.8 from Cornwall Census Project Online

12.1940 - 1949: Truro School and the second World War

1 Speech Day Report 1938-39, p.4
2 The Truronian, July 1939, 15
3 Speech Day Report 1939-40, p.5
4 The Truronian, December 1939, 2
5 Speech Day Report 1939-40, p.5
6 The Truronian, Easter 1942, 2-3
7 The Truronian, December 1941, 4. A.C. Charlesworth, 'Kent College at Truro 1940-45' in Truro School Centenary 1880 – 1980, p.40
8 The Truronian, January 1944, 1
9 The Truronian, Summer 1940, 2, and July 1944, 1
10 The Truronian, December 1941, 2
11 Governors' Minutes 1939 - 1945
12 The Truronian, January 1944, 2

13 The Truronian, December 1945, 5
14 The Truronian, December 1941, 2-3
15 The Truronian, July 1942, 7
16 The Truronian, January 1944, 4
17 The Truronian, December 1945, 7
18 The Truronian, July 1942, 8
19 The Truronian, July 1942, 8
20 The Truronian, Easter 1942,1
21 The Truronian, July 1942, 4
22 The Truronian, Easter 1940, 2
23 From a speech by Hugh Berryman given in 1986 to the Old Boys Association on the golden jubilee of Treliske.
24 The Truronian, Easter 1942, 1
25 'Charles Guest Remembers the Air Raid of 1940' in the Truro School Association Newsletter, February 2000
26 From a speech by Hugh Berryman, 1986
27 Governors' Minutes, December 1940
28 The Truronian, December 1945, 9
29 The Truronian, July 1942, 1
30 The Truronian, Easter 1940, 2
31 The Truronian, July 1944
32 The Truronian, December 1945, 2-3
33 Truro School Memorial Service Booklet, 4 July 1948
34 The Truronian, July 1946, 38, and www.cwgc.org/cwgcsearch the Commonwealth War Graves Commission website
35 The Truronian, July 1942, 2
36 The Truronian, July 1944, 1
37 The Truronian, July 1946, 8
38 The Truronian, December 1945, 1
39 The Truronian, July 1946, 8

13. A.L. Creed

1 G.M. Best, Continuity and Change: A history of Kingswood School 1748 – 1998, p.219
2 The Truronian, December 1945
3 The Truronian, July 1946, 9
4 The Truronian, July 1961, 4
5 Truro School Old Boys Association Newsletter 1973, 8

14. 1950 -1959: Moving On

1 The Truronian, July 1951, 6-7
2 V. Acton and B. Acton, A History of Truro, volume 2: Cathedral City and County Town, p.151

3 The Truronian, December 1954, 3
4 Letter from Nellie Dixon, 1950s.
5 The Truronian, July 1954, 10
6 The Truronian, December 1950, 47
7 The Truronian, July 1952, 54 - 55
8 Ibid, 34
9 The Truronian, December 1956, 30
10 The Truronian, March 1959, 18
11 The Truronian, December 1956, 2, 9
12 The Truronian, March 1955, 6
13 The Truronian, December 1950, 16-17
14 The Truronian, July 1957, 18-19
15 Ibid, 13
16 The Truronian, March 1958, 31
17 The Truronian, July 1956, 52
18 Terraces, 1988, 29
19 The Truronian, July 1953, 16
20 A.L. Creed in Truro School Centenary Booklet 1880-1980, p.45
21 The Truronian, March 1955, 41-42
22 The Truronian, July 1955, 2

15. Derek Burrell
1 S.B. Dawes, 'Valete' in Truro School Association Newsletter, February 2000, from an article in the Methodist Recorder, 20 May 1999
2 D.W. Burrell, 'Methodism and Education in Cornwall' in (ed. S. Foot) Methodist Celebration: A Cornish Contribution (1988), p.71
3 Ibid, p.72
4 Ibid, p.71
5 Dawes, 'Valete' in Truro School Association Newsletter, February 2000
6 Ibid

16. 1960 - 1969: A School for all Seasons
1 The Truronian, July 1960, 28
2 Letter from Tom Magson, dated 30 August 1990.
3 Ibid.
4 The Truronian, July 1960, 29
5 M. A. Bordeaux and J. Bedford Daniel, from addresses at Willday's memorial service, 3 November 1990.
6 The Truronian, July 1968, 5
7 The Truronian, April 1961, 4-5
8 The Truronian, July 1965, 6-7
9 The Truronian, July 1969, 47

10 The Truronian, December, 1961, 1, and July 1962, 3
11 The Truronian, July 1964, 38
12 The Truronian, December 1966, 2
13 The Truronian, December 1964, 23
14 The Truronian, March 1967, 13
15 The Truronian, July 1961, 30, and March 1964, 18
16 The Truronian, April 1962, 66; March 1965, 56, and December 1968, 30
17 The Truronian, March 1964, 14
18 The Truronian, July 1965, 55
19 The Truronian, December 1962, 16; March 1964, 10, 19, and December 1965, 39.
20 The Truronian, July 1964, 43
21 The Truronian, December 1960, 47
22 The Truronian, March 1964, 24-25
23 The Truronian, July 1969, 26
24 The Truronian, July 1964, 39, and July 1969, 12.
25 The Truronian, April 1962, 67
26 The Truronian, April 1963, 20
27 The Truronian, December 1963, 14
28 The Truronian, December 1966, 39

17. 1970 - 1979: The Beginning of Full Independence
1 D. Burrell, in Truro School Centenary Booklet, 1880 – 1980, p.47
2 The Truronian, March 1969, 44
3 D. Burrell in Truro School Old Boys Association Newsletter, February 1973, preface
4 V. Acton and B. Acton, The History of Truro Volume 2: County Town to Cathedral City, p.175, Truro School Old Boys Association Newsletter, February 1973, preface
5 Burrell in Truro School Centenary Booklet, p.47
6 Acton, History of Truro, p.178
7 Burrell, Truro School Centenary Booklet, p.47
8 Terraces, 1977, 50
9 Ibid, 58
10 Terraces, 1978, 20
11 D. Cock, 'Truro's do-it-yourself boys', Methodist Recorder, 29 September 1977, 6, and Western Morning News, 12 September 1977
12 Terraces, 1976, 11-12
13 C. Rowlands, 'The Master Builders', Daily Mail,
30 October 1978
14 Terraces, 1978, 6-9

15 Rowlands, 'The Master Builders',
    30 October 1978,
16 Truro School Centenary Development Appeal
    Pamphlet
17 Terraces, 1980 Centenary Magazine, 38
18 Terraces, 1977, 51
19 Terraces, 1971, 103
20 Terraces, 1975, 88 and 91
21 Terraces, 1976, 22
22 Terraces, 1971, 38; 1977, 71, and 1974, 11
23 Truro School Old Boys Association Newsletter,
    February 1978, 7
24 Terraces, 1972, 107 – 108
25 Terraces, 1974, 36
26 Terraces, 1972, 16
27 Terraces, 1978, 4
28 Terraces, 1976, 3
29 Terraces, 1978, 2-3
30 Terraces, 1972, 110

18. 1980 – 1989: 100 Years and Beyond
1   Truro School Centenary Magazine 1980, 14-16
2   Ibid, 20-28, 47
3   Ibid, 38
4   Ibid, 57
5   Ibid, 61
6   Terraces, 1982, 48
7   Truro School Centenary Magazine 1980, 55
8   Terraces, 1983, 64 -66
9   Terraces, 1987, 4
10 Terraces, 1987, 4 and 16
11 The History Today Companion to British
    History, p.270
12 School Newsletter, March 1986
13 School Newsletter, Summer 1987
14 Terraces, 1984, 3
15 V. Acton and B. Acton, A History of Truro,
    pp. 188 and 195
16 Terraces, 1981, 55
17 Terraces, 1983, 38
18 School Newsletter, Autumn 1988, School
    Newsletter, Autumn 1989
19 School Newsletter, Spring 1989, School
    Newsletter, Summer 1989
20 School Newsletter, Summer 1989
21 Terraces, 1985, 43
22 Terraces, 1981, 71
23 Headmaster's Speech Day Address 1988

24 School Newsletter, Autumn 1988
25 Terraces, 1983, 67
26 Terraces, 1989, 6-7 and 75
27 School Newsletter, December 1986, School
    Newsletter, Spring 1988
28 Terraces, 1989, 29
29 Acton and Acton, A History of Truro p.214

19. Barry Hobbs
1   Terraces, 1993, 3
2   Terraces, 1987, 16
3   Including G.M. Best of Kingswood School, in
    Continuity and Change
4   Terraces, 1991, 31

20. Guy Dodd
1   Terraces, 2002, 5
2   Truro School Newsletter, April 1993
3   Terraces, 2002, 5
4   Terraces, 2002, 5
5   Truro School Newsletter, April 1993

21. 1990 - 1999: Shaking Off the Bonds of Tradition
1   Terraces, 1991, 45
2   Terraces, 1991, 33
3   Terraces, 1991, 30-31
4   Terraces, 1991, 33
5   Terraces, 1994, 34
6   Terraces, 1990, 22
7   Terraces, 1991, 12
8   School Newsletter, Summer 1990
9   Terraces, 1991, 30-31
10 Terraces, 1995, 4-5
11 Acton and Acton, A History of Truro,
    p.224 and 229
12 Acton and Acton, A History of Truro, p.218
13 Terraces, 1994, 23
14 School Newsletter, December 1993
15 Terraces, 1995, 25
16 Terraces, 1998, 51
17 Terraces, 1992, 11
18 Terraces, 1992, 11-12
19 Terraces, 1999, 25-27
20 Terraces, 1999, 61
21 Terraces, 1990, 1
22 Terraces, 1996, 75
23 School Newsletter, July 1993

24 School Newsletter, Summer 1990

25 Terraces, 1997, 35. Terraces, 1998, 10

26 Terraces, 1991, 9 and 30

27 School Newsletter, Summer 1990

28 Terraces, 1994, 42. School Newsletter, December 1994

29 School Newsletter, December 1993. School Newsletter, July 1994

30 Into the Nineties Appeal brochure

31 Terraces, 1991, 30-31

32 Truro School Association Newsletter, February 1998

33 Terraces, 1992, 50

34 V. Acton and B. Acton, A History of Truro, volume 2: County Town to Cathedral City, pp.221 and 225

22. Postscript: 2000-2004

1 Truro School Former Pupils' Association (T.S.F.P.A.) Newsletter, February 2001

2 Terraces, 2000, 106

3 T. S. F. P. A. Newsletter, February 2003

4 Terraces, 2003, 69

5 Terraces, 2002, 8

6 T.S.F.P.A. Newsletter, February 2002

7 Terraces, 2002, 4

8 Terraces, 2004, 168

9 T.S.F.P.A. Newsletter, February 2004

10 T.S.F.P.A. Newsletter, February 2001

11 T.C.M., April 1893, 89

12 T.C.M., July 1892, 4

Famous Former Pupils

1 From notes by J.N. Rosewarne.

2 T.C.M., July 1903

3 Ibid

4 Ibid

5 T.C.M., April 1916, 60

6 West Briton, February 1927

7 From notes by J.N. Rosewarne

8 Ibid

9 N. Baker (ed) Truro School Centenary Booklet, p.53

10 C. Stratton, in T.S.F.P.A. Newsletter, February 2001

11 The Times, 29 August 1978

12 The Truronian, March 1960, 52

13 The Truronian, March 1961

14 The Truronian, April 1963

15 From www.bach-cantatas.com

16 From www.alliedartists.co.uk

17 From Roger Taylor's official website - http://queen-fip.com

18 Truro School Centenary Booklet, p.53

19 Ibid, p.56

20 www2.marksandspencer.com and T.S.F.P.A. Newsletter, February 2003

21 T.S.F.P.A. Newsletter, February 2004

22 West Briton, 23 June 1966

23 Ibid

24 Ibid

25 The Times, 25 December 1986

26 Western Morning News, 23 December 1986

27 Truro School Centenary Booklet, p.53

28 Truro School Centenary, p.53 and Truro School Old Boys Association Newsletter, February 1987

29 T.S.F.P.A. Newsletters, February 2004 and February 2001

30 West Briton, 15 July 2004, T.S.F.P.A. Newsletter February 2002

31 From www.normancroucher.co.uk

32 School Newsletter, Summer 1990

33 Truro School Old Boys Newsletter, February 1991

34 Terraces, 1995, 75

Bibliography

Primary Sources

Notes from J. N. Rosewarne
Letters: T.W.M. Darlington, 1994; J. McCoskrie, 1955; Sir Archibald Marshall to G.O. Vinter, 1964; E.S. Vincent to G. O.Vinter, 1964;
Nellie Dixon, 1950s
Governors' Minutes 1904 – 1910, 1910 – 1915, 1915 – 1923, 1939 – 1945
1924 Inspection Report
Truro School Association Minute Book 1924 – 1950: 'Old Truronians, London'
Speech Day Reports, 1928 -1940
Punishment Book 1936-1943
Truro School Memorial Service Booklet, 4 July 1948
Sir G. P. Christopher, *Through the Years*
1881, 1891 and 1901 English Censuses
Cambridge alumni

School Magazines

Truro College Magazine, 1891 – 1925
The Truronian, 1926 – 1969
Terraces 1970 - 2004
E.Q.V., April 1916
Truro School Old Boys Association Newsletters
Truro School Association Newsletters, 1998-2000
Truro School Former Pupils Association Newsletters, 2001- 2004
School Newsletters, 1959 - 1995

Reference

The History Today Companion to British History (1995)
Kelly's Directory 1883

Newspapers

Royal Cornwall Gazetteer
Cornwall Advertiser
West Briton
Western Morning News
The Times

Websites

www.orcadian.co.uk/features/articles/vanguard.htm - The Orcadian Website
www.gwpda.org/naval/vanguard.htm - Loss of H.M.S. Vanguard
www.cwgc.org/cwgcsearch - the Commonwealth War Graves Commission website
www.bach-cantatas.com
www.alliedartists.co.uk
http://queen-fip.com - Roger Taylor's official website

Secondary Sources

Acton, V. and B. Acton, *A History of Truro: Cathedral City and County Town, volume 2*, (Truro, 2002)
Baker, N., (ed) *Truro School Centenary 1880-1980*, (Truro, 1980)
Barrett, R., *Stately Homes in and around Truro* (Redruth, 1980)
Best, G.M., *Continuity and Change: A History of Kingswood School 1748-1998* (1998)
Burrell, D.W., 'Methodism and Education in Cornwall' in (ed. S. Foot) *Methodist Celebration: A Cornish Contribution* (Redruth, 1988)
Carver, M., *The National Army Museum Book of the Boer War* (1999)
Shaw, T., *A History of Cornish Methodism* (Truro, 1967)
Tangye, M., 'The Wesleyan Methodist Relief Fund for the Cornwall District, 1879' *Old Cornwall* volume 7
Taylor, A.J.P., *History of England 1918 – 1945* (Oxford, 1966)
Williams, D. *Thread of Gold*

Acknowledgements

Thank you to the many people who have helped with the compiling of this book. In particular, thank you to Louise Hillier for her design work; to Lynne Rowland and Hilary Wood for proof reading; and to Robert Cook of the Royal Cornwall Museum in Truro for assistance with photograph research. Also thank you to Truro School, past and present, and the T.S.F.P.A. Committee, especially Steve Floyd, David Johns and George Heyworth for all their help.

Index

Truro School Song

High on the Hill within ... ci...gh...

Would you a-scad to us ... Lis-ten

Chorus.

When we are cold — this is